Against Borders

Off the Fence: Morality, Politics, and Society

The series is published in partnership with the Centre for Applied Philosophy, Politics & Ethics (CAPPE), University of Brighton.

Series Editors:

Bob Brecher, Professor of Moral Philosophy, University of Brighton

Robin Dunford, Senior Lecturer in Globalisation and War, University of Brighton

Michael Neu, Senior Lecturer in Philosophy, Politics and Ethics, University of Brighton

Off the Fence presents short, sharply argued texts in applied moral and political philosophy, with an interdisciplinary focus. The series constitutes a source of arguments on the substantive problems that applied philosophers are concerned with: contemporary real-world issues relating to violence, human nature, justice, equality and democracy, self and society. The series demonstrates applied philosophy to be at once rigorous, relevant, and accessible—philosophy-in-use.

Against Borders

Why the World Needs Free Movement of People

Alex Sager

ROWMAN & LITTLEFIELD
INTERNATIONAL

London • New York

Published by Rowman & Littlefield International Ltd.
6 Tinworth Street, London, SE11 5AL, UK
www.rowmaninternational.com

Rowman & Littlefield International Ltd. is an affiliate of Rowman & Littlefield
4501 Forbes Boulevard, Suite 200, Lanham, Maryland 20706, USA
With additional offices in Boulder, New York, Toronto (Canada), and Plymouth (UK)
www.rowman.com

British Library Cataloguing in Publication Data
A catalogue record for this book is available from the British Library

ISBN: HB 978-1-78660-627-3
        PB 978-1-78660-628-0

Library of Congress Cataloging-in-Publication Data
Library of Congress Control Number: 2019956410

ISBN: 978-1-78660-627-3 (cloth : alk. paper)
ISBN: 978-1-78660-628-0 (pbk. : alk. paper)
ISBN: 978-1-78660-629-7 (electronic)

∞™ The paper used in this publication meets the minimum requirements of
American National Standard for Information Sciences—Permanence of Paper
for Printed Library Materials, ANSI/NISO Z39.48-1992.

Contents

Acknowledgments

This book has benefited from the generosity of hundreds of people, since I began thinking about open borders, beginning in a seminar taught by Ryoa Chung at L'Université de Montréal, and continuing through my doctoral thesis at the University of Calgary, supervised by Dennis McKerlie and Kai Nielsen. Dennis's and Kai's mentorship and guidance were formative and invaluable, and I owe them both a tremendous debt. My committee members Michael Blake, Elizabeth Brake, Antonio Franceschet, Ann Levey, and Mark Migotti all provided valuable feedback and support.

I am thankful to the series editors Bob Brecher, Robin Dunford, and Michael Neu for supporting this project, as well as to Rowman & Littlefield International's editorial team Sarah Campbell, Frankie Mace, and Rebecca Anastasi.

At different stages this manuscript has benefited from advice, comments, and references from Kim Angell, Barbara C. Buckinx, H. G. Callaway, Andreas Cassee, Samuel N. Chambers, Adam Hosein, Avery Kolers, Chris Bertram, Elizabeth Cohen, Phillip Cole, Speranta Dumitru, Jonathan Echeverri Zuluaga, Lior Erez, Bennett Gilbert, Michael James, Matthew Lister, Kieran Oberman, David Owen, José Jorge Mendoza, Gilberto Rosas, Clara Sandelin, Stefan Schlegel, Stephanie Silverman, Andrew Valls, Ashwini Vasanthakumar, Robert Vinten, David Watkins, Mariusz Wegrzyn, and Caleb Yong. I'm particularly grateful to the generosity of Reece Jones and of Michael Neu, who provided detailed comments on many of the chapters.

My parents Ed and Susan Sager have been an unwavering source of support—and of copy editing. Finally, this book would not have been possible without my fellow border crosser, Marifer, who has sustained me these past twenty years with her wisdom, courage, and love. I dedicate it to our daughter Becky in the hope that she will grow in a world with fewer borders.

Introduction

Olive and poultry farmer Cédrik Herrou did not deny that he had smuggled migrants through the Roya valley on the French-Italian border. Nor did he deny that he knew it was illegal. When the judge asked why he did it, Mr. Herrou replied, "There are people dying on the side of the road. It's not right. There are children who are not safe. It is enraging to see children, at 2 in the morning, completely dehydrated" (Nossiter 2017).

Mr. Herrou is not the only person European states have recently prosecuted for helping migrants. Danish rights activist Lisbeth Zornig and her husband Mikael Lindholm were among more than several hundred people recently charged with violating the Danish Aliens Act for transporting people without residence permits. Their crime was to give a family of Syrian refugees a ride from southern Denmark to Copenhagen (Dearden 2016). In the United Kingdom, a group known as the Stansted 15 broke into the Stansted airport and locked themselves in a government-chartered Boeing 767 to block the deportation of sixty migrants to Ghana, Nigeria, and Sierra Leone. Eleven of the passengers scheduled to be deported eventually won appeals to remain legally in the United Kingdom. Nonetheless, the government tried and convicted the Stansted 15 of terrorism (Iqbal 2018; Nathanson 2017). Though the conviction potentially carried a life sentence, Judge Christopher Morgan QC instead imposed suspended sentences and community service, noting that the defendants "didn't have a grievous intent as some may do who commit this type of crime" (Gayle 2019). These prosecutions are not limited to Europe; across the Atlantic, the US government charged volunteers from the humanitarian organization No More Deaths for leaving food and water for migrants in the Arizona desert (Prendergast 2019). It arrested Scott Warren at a humanitarian aid facility and charged him with conspiracy to transport and harbor migrants for providing aid to two migrants, and threatened him with a twenty-year prison sentence. Though the felony trial ended in a hung jury (Devereaux 2019), the US attorney's office intends to retry him for harboring migrants (Associated Press 2019).

Some of these people see themselves as activists resisting what they consider unjust immigration policies. Others have less explicit political motives, instead responding to human need. All are united in their resistance to state policies to prevent movement across borders and to detain and deport members of their communities. A minority of people resisting borders are connected to networks such as the No Border Network or No One Is Illegal that aspire to a world without immigration restrictions.

This book concurs with this open borders minority. It is an extended argument for why we should aspire to a world in which no one is illegal. It aims to contribute to a growing community of activists and scholars calling for opening and even abolishing state borders.[1] We have reached a point in the ethical debates around immigration controls where we are ready to take stock. My hope is that by the end of this book readers will agree that arguments for open borders are among the strongest in political philosophy and applied ethics. The moral case for open borders is analogous to that for women's suffrage, abolition, or LGBT rights, causes which many people violently opposed at the time.

The ethics of immigration is one of the few areas where political philosophy is at the policy vanguard. Though there are vigorous debates about open borders, there is little controversy that many routine practices in immigration enforcement are morally noxious. Enforcement tactics such as workplace raids, immigrant detention (often in for-profit facilities), and outsourcing of migration controls to authoritarian regimes fall far short of principles of proportionality, transparency, and accountability. States actively prevent people from seeking asylum, often committing or abetting human rights violations in the process. They callously fail to resettle the millions of refugees immobilized in camps around the world with no foreseeable opportunity to return to the homes they fled or to integrate into the local society.

I go a step further by not only condemning these practices but also arguing that the appropriate response is open borders. Open borders receive strong support from uncontroversial moral principles:

(1) people matter equally, regardless of their race, gender, ethnicity, religion, or place of birth;
(2) important freedoms should not be curtailed without strong reasons;
(3) rules enforced by state coercion must be justified by giving people under them the opportunity to shape or to contest them; and
(4) we should reform or abolish institutions that systemically oppress, exploit, and harm groups of people.[2]

While these four principles are rejected by some critics of open borders, few philosophers dispute their validity.[3] Rather, their arguments are about how they should be articulated and applied.[4] In my view, if you believe that a commitment to moral equality entails that place of birth should not lead to huge differences in the standard of living, you should support open borders. Similarly, you should be in favor of open borders if you believe in fundamental freedoms such as freedom of movement and the freedoms to pursue one's career, education, and personal life without violent state interference. Open borders are also supported by the democratic conviction that people affected or harmed by policies should have a voice in shaping them. Finally, open borders are the best response to racialized policies that routinely separate families and contribute to migrants suffering physical and sexual abuse and death.

In building my case, I draw on work from within liberal traditions but differ on emphasis. Liberal philosophers have carefully articulated why border controls sit uneasily alongside rights to freedom of movement and opportunity, as well as a commitment to human dignity and equal respect. Much of this discussion, though, has taken place at a level of abstraction divorced from the concrete experience of immigrants and the actual practice of immigration policy and enforcement. In contrast, my arguments give a central place to the violent policing of political borders and how this promotes structural injustice against (often racialized) immigrant groups.

Another way in which my approach differs is that I stress how the terms of debate in the ethics of migration have largely been set by states. Our imaginations fall frequently under the thrall of state-centered ideology. Political philosophers have not adequately engaged social scientific work that has challenged the nation-state-centered worldview (Agnew 1994; Wimmer and Glick Schiller 2003). This means that even opposition to state border controls is set by states: it becomes a denial of a right that states claim to hold. As a result, philosophers have neglected how being an "immigrant" is itself a state-constructed notion, acquiring the meaning of "someone moving into a country" only in the late eighteenth century (Shumsky 2008). It is only possible to be an immigrant in a world in which states categorize people according to their place of birth. This contributes to the uncritical acceptance of morally problematic concepts such as "illegal immigrant."

Furthermore, my goal is to defend open borders not only philosophically but also as a political goal that we have a duty to work toward now. We need to provide reasons why an open-border world is an alternative we can help bring about. Many philosophers writing on immigration assume the justice of fairly extensive border controls on the grounds that open borders are unrealistic, infeasible, or too removed from current policy to require serious consideration (Miller 2016). Another approach is to argue for open borders but as an ideal not meant to guide everyday politics and activism (Carens 2013). I think open borders are a feasible goal and that philosophical arguments for open borders should also serve as a call to political action.

The claim that something is unrealistic often evokes an emotional response, rather than encouraging a clearheaded investigation into reality. It biases us in favor of dominant perceptions of the *status quo*.[5] The infeasibility of open borders is more frequently assumed than argued and the appeal to "realism" is too often a rhetorical trick to dismiss, rather than rebut, opponents. Any attempt to model reality is necessarily selective and involves idealizations, which in turn are more or less defensible in different contexts. We need to justify which facts are salient, which causes are central, which idealizations are merited, what is signal, and what is noise.

In his influential recent book, *Strangers in Our Midst*, David Miller expresses a desire to provide a realistic account of immigration justice. He starts with a fairly uncontroversial account of a realist approach to immigration as one that takes the world as it is, considers evidence from the social sciences, and attempts to provide practical advice to policymakers (Miller 2016: 16–18). Where we part is that he has a worldview that privileges self-contained, homogenous national communities as an axiom for his political philosophy of immigration. Miller prides himself in his hard-headed rejection of fuzzy cosmopolitan hopes for a postnational world and his sympathetic identification with ordinary people rooted to place and bound by custom and language. Unfortunately, as Sarah Fine points out, this identification is based on a fiction, "The idea of the national community, which [in Miller's words] 'conceives of itself as extended in time, indeed often reaching back into antiquity'" (Fine 2017: 721, quoting Miller 2016: 27). Miller frequently conflates actual existing communities with these fictional national communities, asserting a reality for his imagined communities (Anderson 2016) that cannot withstand scrutiny. This leaves much out:

> If we are starting from the world as it is, then we are starting from a world in which existing territorial borders and population distributions have come about in a variety of complex ways, many of which have included extensive injustices, such as those involved in colonialism, slave trading, wars of aggression, ethnic cleansing and land seizures. The list is long. Miller's animating idea of benign, discrete national communities stretching into the past and future allows him to brush over those kinds of facts about the world, at least in this book. (Fine 2017: 723)

The historical injustices and relationships of domination and oppression that Fine describes are ongoing and continue to shape migration. A realist account of the philosophy of migration needs to address this history and study actual political communities, which are not self-contained, culturally homogenous systems. This will affect not only our understanding of migration but also how we evaluate it.

History and political sociology also, in my view, provide support for the possibility of open borders. The current border regime is a recent invention and the degree to which many immigrants are viewed as a security issue and criminalized is even more recent. The study of history teaches us that institutions are contingent and radical change is possible. Moreover, there are many examples of open borders at the local and regional levels, as well as between states in the European Union (EU), Australasia, and South America (Casey 2010). The possibility of bringing them about entails a moral imperative to support open borders.

Chapter 1 clarifies what I mean by open borders. Too often debates about border controls falter because parties disagree about what is proposed. Articulating an open-border policy requires delving into the nature of borders and the ways in which they encourage, prevent, and regulate mobility. This serves to dispel misconceptions about open borders and what they entail, enabling a more fruitful discussion.

The next three chapters present major arguments for open borders. Chapter 2 surveys ethical arguments for open borders based on freedom and the need to justify coercion. Chapter 3 supplements these arguments with arguments based on the demands of distributive justice. It shows how border controls not only maintain inequalities across territories but also actively serve to stratify populations, promoting inequitable distributions of opportunities and resources. It connects the case for open borders to structural injustice, often inflicted against racialized groups. Chapter 4 moves from more abstract philosophical principles of freedom and equality to the practice of immigration enforcement, again in the context of structural injustice. I contend that even if rights and equality do not require open borders in theory, a careful assessment of immigration enforcement makes them a practical requirement for justice.

Chapter 5 challenges common objections that justify immigration restrictions by appealing to the right to self-determination and the concern that open borders would threaten security, endanger environmental sustainability and measures to reduce or regulate population. Chapter 6 turns to justifications for restricting immigration on cultural grounds and because immigration will threaten the welfare state by reducing social trust. It also disputes the infeasibility of open borders. Chapter 7 connects the book's arguments to questions of political action and personal responsibility for migrants, citizens, media, and academics. Migrants are morally justified in resisting border controls and Cédrik Herrou, Lisbeth Zornig, Mikael Lindholm, the Stansted 15, and Scott Warren should be praised for their moral courage. It also means that most of us are culpable in supporting or remaining complacent about today's migration regimes. If we aspire to a just world, we need to do our part in working toward open borders.

NOTES

1. A partial list of recent books on open borders includes Bauder (2017); Cole (2000); Carens (2013); Jones (2016; 2019); and Walia (2013). Open-border coverage has become increasingly common in major media outlets (Manjoo 2019; Miron 2018; Washington 2019) and a multidisciplinary, scholarly literature has flourished.

2. Joseph Carens (1987) demonstrated this in "Aliens and Citizens: The Case for Open Borders," showing that Rawlsian egalitarian, libertarian, and utilitarian theories all provide strong reasons for supporting open borders.

3. Useful overviews of the ethics of immigration include Bauder (2015), Seglow (2005), Wellman (2015), and Wilcox (2009).

4. For example, both David Miller and Michael Blake argue against open borders. Nonetheless, Miller adopts what he calls a "weak cosmopolitanism," which accepts the equal moral worth of human beings and the obligation of states to do their fair share to respect human rights (Miller 2016), and Michael Blake (2013b) argues, "We Are All Cosmopolitans Now." The view that states can dismiss the interests of outsiders (e.g., Borjas 2001) does not withstand moral scrutiny. The stipulation that there is no need to take the rights and interests of would-be immigrants into consideration is to deny their equal moral worth.

5. For an important discussion on the limitations of crude distinctions between realism and idealism and the need to take a more critical approach to what describes the real world, see Sandelind (2019).

Chapter 1

What Are Open Borders?

Open borders are anathema to respectable company, a sign of unrealistic radicalism or of mushy idealism. A January 30, 2018, Fact Sheet from the White House begins: "For the past decade, attempts at immigration reform have failed because open borders special interests in both parties have dominated the discussion" (White House 2018a). Later in the year, the White House went on to accuse Congressional Democrats of "furthering their agenda of open borders and trying to release all illegal alien families and minors who show up at the border" (White House 2018b). The Trump administration used the charge of an open borders agenda to deflect public outrage from their policy of separating children from their parents. Instead of honoring the United States' own asylum laws and releasing families with credible fear of persecution into the community, they chose to identify opposition to traumatic detention and family separation with open borders.

False accusations that Democrats support open borders were a mainstay of Trump's campaign and continued during his presidency. Indeed, "open borders" has become a metonym for any proposed immigration reform that threatens to make the current immigration system less brutal or more inclusive. In reality, open borders is not a mainstream political cause, even among people sharply critical of the current immigration system. The idea that Congressional Democrats advocate open borders has no basis in reality (Yglesias 2018).[1]

Nor are open borders particularly respected in academia, where many social scientists feel obliged to distinguish their progressive policy recommendations from open borders.[2] Leading migration scholar Hein de Haas captures the unofficial consensus on open borders among mainstream researchers. Since states need to define their membership to collect taxes and to provide public services, Haas tells us, "It would therefore be foolish to argue that countries should just 'open their borders' by allowing everybody to immigrate and settle." He scolds open-borders advocates as "naive" in their failure to recognize that "modern states need to establish rules about entry, stay and citizenship." Instead, we must recognize "the false opposition between closed and open borders" (Haas 2016) and understand that immigration policies are a matter of selection, rather than blunt inclusion or exclusion.

Haas makes some cogent points. The opposition between "open" and "closed" borders is simplistic and unhelpful to describe actual migration policies and patterns. States need to define who is a member to determine rights to public services and obligations to contribute. This requires policies that classify people. Nonetheless, this does not mean that we should reject open borders. As I will show in this book, open borders are neither the dreaded *coco* (the Latin American bogeyman) that right-wing politicians summon to frighten constituents nor the irresponsible fantasy of dewy-eyed globalists.

Why then are so many commentators on open borders apocalyptic or dismissive? People arguing for or against border controls too often avoid analyzing the nature and function of borders. Many objections against open borders gain their plausibility from a distorted view about what open borders entail. While critics are partly responsible for constructing an open borders straw man, many open borders theorists give only cursory attention to the nature of borders and fail to articulate their vision clearly. They present moral reasons for opening borders, leaving implicit the question of what borders are and what opening them would entail. As a result, open borders don't receive a fair hearing.

SOME REMARKS ON BORDERS

The popular imagination identifies borders with lines on a map, demarcating the space between two territories. On this account, a border is a line in the sand—or, better yet, a wall—designed to exclude (Parker and Vaughan-Williams 2012). This view supports a vision of sovereignty and immigration enforcement that has little to do with reality.

To determine how open borders should be, we need to know what they are. The challenge is that the nature and functions of borders prove surprisingly elusive.[3] At a high level of abstraction, borders are lines that mark and divide space and people. They allow us to classify the world, permitting geographical and social distinctions. Though borders may be physically constituted by rivers or mountains or constructed from steel or concrete, their existence as *borders* derives from the fact that people represent them as such. While some borders may be chosen because of their geological features, their status as borders derives from people's choices. The Rio Grande forms part of the

US-Mexico border because the US and Mexican governments recognize it as doing so. The Kitimat River in the Canadian Northwest is not a national border because nobody sees it as one.

Recognition is fundamental. Politicians sometimes pretend that borders can be imposed unilaterally, but state borders depend on international recognition. The importance of international recognition is most obvious when groups contest state borders or attempt to secede. Nonstate borders—and most borders are nonstate borders—also require acknowledgment. Belonging to an ethnicity or religion—two salient instances of social membership—depends on (sometimes fraught) mutual recognition. Borders are often established by conventions, sustained by most people's (often tacit) agreement to abide by them. A border rejected by a significant number of people is at best unstable; at worst, it is not a border at all.

Borders cannot be separated from their representation. They come into existence when people acknowledge them (Balibar 2002; Novak 2017). Another way of putting this is that borders are in important respects socially constructed. Even navigating physical barriers depends on technology and knowledge. Traversing a mountain range turns from an ordeal to a scenic tour with a helicopter. Bolt cutters transform an unguarded barbed wire fence from barrier into a nuisance. While walls may reassure a nervous electorate, passports and visas are more effective impediments to mobility; without these documents, most people can never approach the territory.

The socially constructed nature of borders alerts us to the danger of naturalizing state borders, treating their current structure as inevitable. State borders are not natural features of the world. They are the result of political and legal decisions that in turn rest on the widespread agreement that these decisions are legitimate—or, at least, that they will be effectively enforced. The East German authorities' decision not to stop people from leaving in 1989 led to the border's quick dissolution.

One reason why state borders are often seen as natural is methodological nationalism, a cognitive bias in which the world is perceived from the perspective of states. States promote a state-centered epistemology in which nation-states are taken as the primary unit of analysis and national territories are treated as self-sufficient containers (Wimmer and Glick Schiller 2002). Transnational connections and identities are effaced and society is reduced to national communities that do not reflect the diverse people who live in the territory. Through nation-building, state borders often come to appear inevitable or, at least, the only reasonable or legitimate boundaries for political, social, and legal groups (Sager 2016a).

Borders also determine how we represent the world, marking off the categories that allow us to make sense of our physical and social environments. Borders simultaneously determine their representation as we represent them.

Categories such as nation-states, ethnic groups, races, genders, religions, and social classes help people make sense of the buzzing, blooming confusion of the social world. They are necessary, but can also be pernicious, imposing epistemically unwarranted and ethically noxious features on individuals and groups (Brubaker 2002).

Borders are social constructions; this doesn't make them any less real. Borders constitute our world. Gerrymandered boundaries place unpopular politicians in office. Trade barriers affect the success and failure of businesses. Thousands of immigrants die trying to cross national borders every year (International Organization for Migration n.d.). Moreover, borders play a central role in what Ian Hacking calls "making up people" (Hacking 2004). The possibility of being black, white, or Asian, Peruvian, Ethiopian, or Dutch, gay, straight, or pansexual, depends on borders that demarcate these as categories in the social world.

The socially constructed nature of borders helps explain why the refrain, "What part of illegal don't you understand?" falls flat. Immigration laws are choices and the ways states classify immigrants vary. The classifications have not always existed and have changed significantly in recent decades. Immigration reformers insist that the current laws are unjust and should be abolished or changed. They may be mistaken but to dismiss their insistence of the injustice of immigration law based on the illegality of illicitly crossing borders begs the question. The open borders debate is about the justice of immigration restrictions and the need to change the nature of state borders. Ultimately, it is a question of categorization: open-borders advocates want a world where there is no category under which migrants are labeled illegal.

When we naturalize borders, treating them as part of the fabric of the world, we obscure another important part of their nature. Borders are best understood as processes, not as things. As critical border studies theorists have shown, we shouldn't conceive of borders as fixed, static lines but rather look at them in terms of the practices that produce and sustain them (Parker and Vaughan-Williams 2009: 586). It is not so much borders but rather the bordering process that affects our lives (Newman 2006: 144, cf. 148). Wall building is political theater, dangerous only because it distracts us from the vast network of state and nonstate agents that police human mobility.

Borders form part of the techniques that states and other actors use to exercise power over people (Walters 2011). Sometimes this power is stark. Immigration and Customs Enforcement (ICE) agents round up poultry workers at gunpoint and detain them for deportation (Hing 2009). This displays the state's power over its population, especially over immigrants without authorization to live and work in the territory. (Though by no means exclusively—in the United States, citizenship is not a guarantee against deportation [Bier 2018].) Border enforcement is, among other things, a spectacle to proclaim the state's power to exclude, a proclamation that may diverge from the real power to do so and may in fact mask the inclusion of exploited immigrants with few rights and subordinate status (De Genova 2013).

In many other cases, the power exercised over people is subtler or disguised. The power to shape borders is the power to classify and, through classification, to include and exclude. Parker and Vaughan-Williams write about how modern political subjects are "bordered" through documents such as passports, identity cards, social security numbers, and drivers' licenses that determine their belonging (2012). Borders mark social categories and legal statuses such as citizen, permanent resident, temporary worker, student, and undocumented immigrant. These categories determine rights and opportunities. This in turn affects how people come to see each other and themselves. Some immigrants without legal authorization to be in the United States internalize categories of "good immigrants" who work hard, obey the law, and deserve to remain, and "bad immigrants" who lack work ethic, break laws, and deserve deportation (Andrews 2018).

Another common misconception is that the primary function of borders is exclusion. Borders are porous. How porous they are and who can cross them varies widely. Borders can exclude, but they also connect groups and facilitate movement. Many borders are more like doors than walls. Doors can be shut, but their purpose is to regulate and structure mobility, not to prevent it. A door to a private home keeps out strangers but also directs family and friends into the foyer. While it is easy to focus on mobility restrictions, it is perhaps more remarkable how many people cross borders. Airports are sites of exclusion where people without authorized travel documents are turned away. But they also facilitate the travel of millions of people every day. According to the US Department of Transportation's Bureau of Transportation Statistics, there were 223.4 million passengers on international flights to and from the United States in 2017.[4] Hein de Haas, Katharina Natter, and Simona Vezzoli's analysis shows that immigration policies have actually grown less restrictive since 1945, though there is considerable variation over categories of immigration (Haas, Natter, and Vezzoli 2018). This reveals a discursive gap between tough-talking politicians and policies that allow for considerable mobility. Nonetheless, the fact that some people can travel with ease while others must risk their lives with smugglers raises questions of justice.

Finally, we should ask: *where is the border?*[5] (Johnson et al. 2011; Jones and Johnson 2014). Borders are often represented as lines that clearly demarcate an inside and outside. There is some truth to this, but matters are complicated. While official territorial boundaries may have symbolic significance, border enforcement extends far beyond the edges of political jurisdictions, reaching into the interior of states, outward into other states, and inward, forming people's identities. While border control regimes are often present at official borders, their reach is much more extensive. In most cases they include internal enforcement through deportations and external enforcement through measures designed to prevent people from reaching states' legal territories (e.g., through maritime interception). Border enforcement is frequently offshored, with the Australian government outsourcing indefinite immigrant detention to Nauru and Manus Island, and the EU outsourcing enforcement to Libya to prevent refugees from claiming asylum on European territory (Amnesty International 2016; Andersson and Keen 2019; Gleeson 2016). Private and public border enforcements are intertwined, with for-profit prisons and security companies playing a central role.

Border controls are often portrayed as exclusively directed at people outside of the community. In fact, they are often enforced internally, against immigrants, but also against people identified as immigrants (Mendoza 2016a). In the United States, green card holders remain vulnerable to deportation for minor offenses even if they came to the country as children, have lived in the country for decades, and/or have close family ties within the country. These immigrants often serve prison sentences before they are remanded to immigration detention, then further punished by exile, sometimes to countries they have not seen since early childhood. Nor are racialized US citizens exempt from the threat of deportation. ICE continues to reenact the ignominious history of mass deportations of Mexicans in the 1930s today (Balderrama and Rodriguez 2006).

In sum, borders are constructed in complex and diverse ways, often with morally problematic consequences. Borders are produced by human choices and sustained by human recognition. When they harm, oppress, or exploit people, we should change or abolish them.

WHAT OPEN BORDERS ARE
(AND WHAT THEY ARE NOT)

These remarks on the nature of borders help clarify the book's central question: Why should we have open borders? To answer this question, we need to know what open borders mean. Succinctly put, open-borders proponents advocate abolishing borders that use force to produce illegality. To support open borders is to deny that the use of a state coercion to restrict immigration into state territories is ethical. Immigrants, irrespective of their place of birth, ethnic affiliation, religion, political affiliation, or economic status should be free to visit, work, and settle in any country. It rejects the rights of states to create categories of people defined by their limited access to the rights allotted to citizens, including rights to work and to remain in the territory where one lives.

The state's role in categorizing people in ways that produce illegal statuses is at the core of the debate. Journalists and scholars have debated the appropriate terminology for immigrants who have violated an immigration law by crossing a border or residing in a territory without permission. Perhaps the most problematic of these terms is *illegal alien* or *illegal immigrant*, giving rise to the slogan *No Human Is Illegal*. Illegality is a property that should apply to actions, not persons. A less pejorative term is "undocumented immigrant," which is inaccurate. "Undocumented" describes what immigrants lack—documents—rather than the condition of people excluded from work, public services, education, and living in constant fear of deportation (Bauder 2014). Some scholars have opted for the seemingly more neutral terms "unauthorized" or "irregular immigrant" (Carens 2013: 129–30).

This is an improvement, but the most appropriate expression is "illegalized immigrant," which draws attention to the process in which people are made illegal (Bauder 2014; Dauvergne 2008). Only some borders produce illegality. Producing illegality generally requires a state willing to enforce immigration regulations with the threat of force. State borders are maintained through what Cecilia Menjívar and Leisy J. Abrego call legal violence—violence that has structural and symbolic aspects "embedded in legal practices, sanctioned, actively implemented through formal procedures, and legitimated—and consequently seen as 'normal' and natural because it 'is the law'" (Menjívar and Abrego 2012: 1387).

Whether or not state borders produce illegality is a choice. How they do it is also a choice. Legal scholars describe the merger of immigration law with criminal law as "crimmigration" (García Hernández 2013; Stumpf 2006). Since 2006, the United States has greatly expanded the list of crimes—including misdemeanors and immigration violations—that lead to deportation and exponentially expanded the use of immigrant detention (Nethery and Silverman 2015). Criminalization creates a vicious cycle in which legal categories and sanctions justify harsh treatment of immigrants and communicate that immigration is primarily a matter of security, rather than economics, family unification, or hospitality.

The open-borders position has proven easy to misunderstand. The case for open borders is not a case against the jurisdictional boundaries of the territorial state. It does not deny that states have a legal and moral right to make and enforce laws over a territory (though this right is restricted by considerations of justice). Rather, open-borders advocates oppose states' right to impose regimes of control over people's movement in and out of the territory and their exclusion of groups of people from political membership.

This position is distinct from moderate calls for more humane borders that leave much of the current border regime in place. It also differs from more radical calls for no borders that demand the abolition or, at least, the radical transformation of the state system and of capitalism. Finally, it is distinct from libertarian and utilitarian cases for open borders that are willing to compromise access to public benefits for more generous immigration policies. People have a right to travel freely across national territories, to settle, and to acquire full membership that entitles them to the same rights and benefits as everyone else (as well as corresponding responsibilities).

Most people critical of the current immigration regimes are not open-borders advocates and in fact distance themselves from what they see as politically unviable if not pernicious radicalism. Open-borders advocates may ally with people fighting for more humane borders. Nonetheless, they need to take care not to allow humanitarianism to legitimize immigration restrictions. Open borders does not mean more open borders; rather, it entails that people can move freely across state lines and settle abroad regardless of their citizenship.

Open borders is distinct from its more radical cousin no borders (Anderson et al. 2009; Bauder 2015; King 2016). No-borders advocates seek to dismantle many of the borders that define our lives in favor of radically democratic associations (Chamberlain 2016). No-borders advocates often connect their work to revolutionary change by opposing capitalism and class hierarchy and moving toward commonly owned property and radical democratic communities. For no-borders advocates, migration justice requires radical, systemic change. They often see the nation-state system as inherently corrupt. State borders, even if opened, would continue to perpetuate oppressive and inequitable relationships. In more radical camps, open borders are sometimes seen as part of the neoliberal deregulation of markets and destruction of social safety nets, shifting state violence and oppression to the private sector.

No-borders advocates do not literally reject all borders. They at least accept borders established by mutual agreement, though it is often unclear how they negotiate cases in which members of the group wish to exclude others seeking admission. David Newman points out that we cannot even imagine a borderless world: "Even the globalization purists would accept that the basic ordering of society requires categories and compartments, and that borders create order" (Newman 2006: 143). Nonetheless, social and political units under a no-borders politics would be very different from the *status quo*.

The case for open borders is less ambitious. I do not necessarily argue for the need to fundamentally reshape major political, economic, and social institutions (though, importantly, I do not argue against it). I follow Joseph Carens in presupposing a world of sovereign states governing discrete territories (though it is important to recognize that this model of the world is a considerable simplification) (Carens 2013: 231). My defense of open borders focuses on coercively enforced state borders that exclude people outside of the political community as well as segregate and allow for the policing of illegalized populations within state borders (along with populations that may have legal status but are associated with illegalized populations because of ethnicity, nationality, or social class). State borders are not by any means the only morally problematic types of borders, but a moral assessment of borders more generally is beyond the scope of this book.[6]

Open borders does not simply entail a right to travel and to work. People within the territory are entitled to full membership upon establishing residence, and the process of establishing residence should be short and more or less automatic. Immigrants should not be treated differently in the countries where they settle—after a short period of time, they should receive the same economic, social, and political rights that long-standing residents enjoy. Political membership should be granted through residence; residence in turn creates civic duties and responsibilities.[7] To allow free movement across national frontiers but to treat immigrants differently from citizens is simply to move the border inside the territory. The insistence on settlement distinguishes my account from proposals that allow for labor movement but exclude immigrants from important civil and human rights.

While my account of open borders is conservative in leaving the existing state system largely intact, at least for the time being, it needs to be distinguished from some market-based arguments. Economic arguments support a case for much more open borders. Border restrictions violently curtail opportunities, upholding an international regime that Joseph Carens has compared to feudal birthright privilege (Carens 1987). Nonetheless, we need to take care when presenting economic evidence supporting open borders. A persistent danger in refuting anti-immigrant pundits who claim that immigration harms domestic workers is that it risks allowing them to set the terms of debate. As Nick Gill puts it,

> Some myths circulated in conservative texts concerning the potential negative implications of No Borders are dangerous not only from the point of view of their *prima facie* inaccuracy, but also because they seek to engage critics on a discursive terrain that takes for granted the ethical license to discuss foreigners in instrumental terms. (Gill 2009: 115)

What holds for no borders also holds for open borders. Economic research is important and necessary, and books such as Jason Riley's *Let Them In: The Case for Open Borders* and Philip Legraine's *Immigrants: Your Country Needs Them* effectively refute conservative myths about immigrants taking jobs; it is nonetheless the case that these refutations allow conservative alarmists to determine the terms of engagement (Gill 2009; see Legrain 2007; Riley 2008).

In particular, many pro-immigrant arguments adopt a nationalist and, arguably, neoliberal framework, insisting that immigrants benefit the state, spurring innovation, creating jobs, or doing work that natives refuse. These arguments accept, if sometimes only implicitly, that immigration policy should be driven by national self-interest. Economic arguments are instrumental arguments. They support immigration because economic research largely indicates the positive effects of immigration. Nonetheless, basing our attitudes or policies on immigration because of its effects allows opponents to maintain that should immigration have negative effects, then closing borders is warranted. This is at least part of the reason why so much attention is paid to research that suggests immigration has small negative effects on (at least some) domestic workers' wages[8] and to the claim that skilled emigration ("brain drain") harms people who stay behind (Sager 2016b).

Immigrants are regularly portrayed as security threats, criminals, welfare recipients who simultaneously "steal" jobs and much else. Research shows a weakly negative relationship between immigration and crime (Light and Miller 2018; Ousey and Kubrin 2018) and a largely positive economic impact (Organization for Economic Cooperation and Development 2013). Nonetheless, it is dangerous to represent immigrants as unusually virtuous, hardworking, entrepreneurial, and patriotic, playing into a dynamic of "good" immigrants who deserve an opportunity and "bad" immigrants who deserve detention and deportation.

The case for open borders presented here does not depend on immigrants benefiting domestic economies or their moral virtue or outstanding character. Rather, it proceeds from fundamental moral principles concerning freedom and equality, from duties to not unjustly inflict harm (including the harm of using violence to prevent people from seizing opportunities), and the harms of domination, exploitation, and oppression.

AN OPEN-BORDER POLICY

Residents of Vancouver, Washington, frequently drive across the Interstate Bridge that spans the Columbia River into Portland, Oregon. They come for work, to study, to visit friends, or to shop. Some of them decide to relocate, taking up residence in Portland. There are no gates or checkpoints blocking the Interstate Bridge. No Oregon Border Patrol officers in paramilitary gear detain and deport people without the proper paperwork.

The Washington-Oregon border is open. Nonetheless, there is a border. Washington residents who have never been to Oregon will quickly learn that there is no sales tax. They will be unpleasantly surprised that, unlike Washington, Oregon has income tax. If they apply to an Oregon university before establishing residence, they will pay significantly higher tuition. But once they live the majority of twelve consecutive months in Oregon, they become Oregon residents with all of the benefits and burdens this entails. Like most cities, Portland uses residence to establish membership and to hold elections, provide public services, and collect taxes. This refutes Yael Tamir's insistence that "when individuals move freely and frequently in and out of a democratic system, it will become unclear who is entitled to vote and who is entitled to be elected" (Tamir 2019: 33). In her view, "The concept of an 'open border' is an oxymoron; borders are meant to be closed, to draw a distinction between what is in and what is out; crossing the border must be the exception and not the rule" (Tamir 2019: 34).

The examples of moving between territorial units within nation-states show that to argue for open borders is not to argue against establishing any borders or bounded communities. Rather, it is to argue against the ways that some borders are constituted. It is neither feasible nor desirable to eliminate all borders or forms of closure—at the very least, few of us would wish to give up the borders that shape our families and intimate friendships. Furthermore, geography is inescapable. Whatever political units one prefers, politics—and life—needs to take place somewhere. Borders are a tool for organizing territory and for regulating flows. It is possible to change how borders function, what they include and exclude, and how they are enforced without dissolving them. The question isn't whether or not to have borders or whether all borders should be open but rather which borders we want to sustain and how open they should be. Open-borders proponents focus on state borders; they are not committed to opening borders around family and personal lives.

Many of the arguments for closing state borders can be deflected by showing that, even in a world in which states do not police mobility, borders that have moral value can be preserved. For example, the fear that community and culture will be undermined by high levels of immigration neglects the many ways in which communities and cultures are sustained in diverse metropolises. Identity and solidarity can be achieved without legally enforced borders. In fact, most borders around communities are not established or maintained through state violence but rather through free association and informally enforced norms.

This connects to another important point: there is little reason to think that open borders would undermine sovereignty. State sovereignty is multidimensional, involving first, the juridical equality between states that allows them to join international organizations and to enter into agreement with other states; second, the right to exclude other states from intervening on their territory; third, the right to administrate activities within state borders; and, fourth, the ability to control the movement of goods, capital, and people across borders

(Krasner 1999). Open borders for migrants would only primarily affect the fourth dimension of sovereignty (Krasner 1999: 13); they would leave states' abilities to exclude foreign political actors from their territories or even to regulate the movement of goods or capital largely untouched.

The open-borders position is that individuals should be able to move and settle around the world, joining states as members of equal status. It should not be conflated with state-sponsored colonialism or what Kelly Greenhill calls "weaponized migration" in which states use migration as a foreign policy tool (2010). Conflating all migration with settler colonialism unfairly treats human mobility as pathological and mischaracterizes the vast majority of migrants as usurpers. It also ignores the experience of colonized people, many who have turned to migration as a response to dispossession (Sharma and Wright 2008). The problem with "weaponized migration" (an alarming expression that gives too much credence to dystopic narratives of migrant invasions) is not migration but state violence forcing people to move.

A more general argument against open borders rests on communities' right to self-determination (Walzer 1983; Wellman 2008). It is possible that the addition of new members could reduce the power of current residents to shape the political and cultural fabric in ways they prefer. In a democratic state, immigrants would become part of the franchise with a right to a voice in political decisions. But even with open borders, states would continue to exercise authority over their legal, educational, and administrative institutions within their territory. A change in the composition of political subjects through immigration does not undermine sovereignty any more than women's suffrage or abolition did in the past—or the addition of new members when children come of age does today. Open borders largely leave the structure of the nation-state in place.

Another reason why open borders would not undermine sovereignty is that opening borders does not mean that human mobility cannot be regulated in any way. Open borders mean that, under most circumstances, states cannot prevent people from entering and settling in the territory—moving from Sri Lanka to Canada would be akin to moving from Washington to Oregon. Nonetheless, freedom of movement is not absolute, even leaving aside considerations of security or public health. Under most accounts, private property places significant limits on freedom of movement within states, though these limits should be open to challenge. Similarly, some public spaces may be justly closed at times. Just as mobility within states can be regulated, regulation of international mobility can be compatible with open borders. People can be directed to ports of entry and there may be circumstances where entry could justly be delayed. Even with open borders, there will still need to be processes to determine residence, though these processes should be easily accessible and fairly automatic. What is crucial for the open-borders question, though, is that mobility restrictions need to be justified to everybody, regardless of their citizenship or place of birth.

Furthermore, critics of open borders often conflate the achievement of open borders with their implementation. Advocating for open borders doesn't mean implementing them overnight. To support open borders does not mean immediately removing any border restrictions, regardless of the consequences. Even those of us who think that the potential dangers of open borders are overstated can agree that, at the very least, there are questions of coordination that need to be dealt with before throwing open the gates. Any reasonable implementation plan for open borders would likely phase them in over time.

Finally, there is no conflict between open borders and a right to stay home (Oberman 2011) or with substantial place-based rights and duties (Ochoa 2016). Though opening borders would play an important role in poverty alleviation, it is not meant to substitute for other measures or absolve states of responsibility toward people within their territories. Achieving open borders would be a significant and indeed necessary step toward a more just world; it is nonetheless far from sufficient. Politics and community will continue to be based in physical spaces (though the nature of space is complex and in many cases transnational or dispersed across territories). What changes under open borders is not the importance of place but that more places become accessible to more people.

This chapter clarified what open borders mean and entail. We cannot argue for open borders without explicitly identifying what we are arguing for. At least some disagreement around open borders is a result of interlocutors talking past each other because they have different conceptions about what open borders are. The next three chapters canvass the major arguments for why we should support open borders. In these chapters, I show that the case for open borders is overdetermined: there are multiple strong reasons for open borders that can be grouped under freedom, equality, and the severe harms and systemic injustice caused by the imposition of immigration regimes. The first and in some respects most straightforward cluster of arguments for open borders is based on freedom. This is the topic of the next chapter.

NOTES

1. Reacting to the horror of very young children torn from their parents, a few Democrats did call for abolishing Immigration and Customs Enforcement (ICE). Abolishing ICE, an agency that dates back to post-9/11 legislation in 2013 and, unlike the Border Patrol, does not in fact operate at the US borders, is quite different from calling for open borders (Farley 2018).

2. An example of this is Josiah Heyman's *Finding a Moral Heart for U.S. Immigration Policy*, which presents a radical vision of immigration in which decisions are made at the local level and shifts the role of immigration agencies to coordination, rather than restriction. Much of Heyman's vision is congruent with open borders. Nonetheless, Heyman states that he does "not propose open borders, but rather to use the boundary as a registration point for the regulation of flows" (1998: 70).

3. The term "border" is connected to a variety of other terms: boundaries, frontiers, lines, limits, and edges. Sometimes the use of the term "borders" is limited to territorial (especially state) boundaries. Though a precise definition of terms can be useful for the purposes of analysis, there is no universally agreed upon terminology and, in practice, they overlap.

4. See United States Department of Transportation, Bureau of Transportation Statistics https://www.bts.gov/newsroom/2017-traffic-data-us-airlines-and-foreign-airlines-us-flights. Last accessed October 30, 2019.

5. Another important topic concerns how borders are temporarily defined—the tourist after a period of time becomes an unauthorized immigrant (Cohen 2018).

6. I make some preliminary remarks about how we might address this question in chapter 5 of *Toward a Cosmopolitan Ethics of Mobility* (Sager 2018c).

7. I ignore for the moment the complications that arise for people with multiple residences and transnational connections. There may be additional reasons for people to retain rights in territories where they maintain close connections. See Bauböck (2007), for discussion.

8. See the exchanges between Card (1990); Borjas (2015); and Clemens and Hunt (2019).

Chapter 2

Freedom, Coercion, and Open Borders

Li Yifeng calls himself a "born border crosser," but his two attempts to escape China by crossing illegally into Myanmar and Hong Kong failed. Interviewed shortly after his release from a detention center in the southern city of Shenzhen, he says:

> The pursuit of freedom is the hardest thing in this world. In China, if you are dying of hunger, nobody gives a damn. But when you try to move to a new place to find food for yourself and look for a change of lifestyle, someone will immediately pounce and arrest you. In places such as Europe, the U.S., and Australia, people claim they have democracy and freedom. But the governments there will not grant entry to you if you don't have money or if you don't qualify as a political refugee. No matter how many times you tell them that you love democracy and freedom, they still don't give a damn. It's so damn hypocritical. (Liao 2009: 251)

Li Yifeng is correct. Places such as Europe, the United States, and Australia claim to endorse democracy and freedom. But their alleged commitment to democracy and freedom cannot be reconciled with their immigration policies and practices. The bulwark of liberal democracy—at least as it is conceived by its supporters—capsizes against the illiberal treatment of foreigners.[1] Open borders are needed to remove the hypocrisy of states that claim to love freedom and democracy but build physical and virtual walls to keep people out.

One of the most fundamental freedoms is freedom of movement. The goal of this chapter is to demonstrate that a commitment to freedom of movement entails a right to immigrate, to move freely across state borders and to settle in the territory.

FREEDOM OF MOVEMENT AND A RIGHT
TO IMMIGRATE

In her address for the Lessing Prize of the Free City of Hamburg, Hannah
Arendt tells us:

> Of all the specific liberties which may come into our minds when we hear the
> word "freedom," freedom of movement is historically the oldest and also the
> most elementary. Being able to depart for where we will is the prototypical
> gesture of being free, as limitation of freedom of movement has from time
> immemorial been the precondition for enslavement. Freedom of movement is
> also the indispensable precondition for action, and it is in action that men pri-
> marily experience freedom in the world. (Arendt 1959: 9; quoted in De Genova
> 2010: 33)

Arendt's address, "On Humanity in Dark Times: Thoughts about Lessing" is
only tangentially about freedom of movement. Rather, it is about the German
critic, dramatist, and philosopher Gotthold Ephraim Lessing's *Selbstdenken*,
"thinking for oneself" and its relationship to action and to the dark times
Arendt lived through. Ultimately, Arendt's speech is about friendship and the
public search for truth.

Nonetheless, Arendt's statement on freedom of movement captures important truths. Action depends on mobility and many of our goals and plans rely
on it. The High Commission for Human Rights observes, "Liberty of movement is an indispensable condition for the free development of a person"
(Office of the High Commission for Human Rights 1999). Our ability to
make a living, to pursue opportunities, and to maintain relationships depends
on significant freedom of movement, as do attending school, searching for a
job, or remaining with family. Even rights like freedom of religion and conscience have important connections to freedom of movement. Religious pil-
grimages require travel. Democracy depends on a significant right to freedom
of movement, not least because freedom of association and assembly requires
it. Authoritarian regimes restrict movement to crush popular resistance and
political organization, imposing checkpoints and curfews and refusing to
allow people to gather in public spaces. In extreme cases, the ability to move
freely is needed to escape danger or persecution.

This leads to another reason for why freedom of movement has a central
place in the pantheon of rights: it is a necessary condition for exercising most
other rights. Individual rights are bound together in mutually reinforcing
systems. Equal opportunity is impossible without freedom from discrimination; the right to due process guards against arbitrary detention. Rights
establish preconditions that open a space for human freedom and well-being.
Since they are not exercised in isolation, removing one right has far-reaching

implications for other rights. As Antoine Pécoud and Paul de Guchteneire put it, "Elaborating a right to mobility is not about adding one more right to a long list of rights; rather, it is about fostering respect for existing human rights" (Pécoud and de Guchteneire 2006: 76).

Freedom of movement is also something people value in itself. As Maurice Cranston observes, we move for the sake of moving:

> One of the things that is meant by saying that men have a natural right to free-dom of movement is to assert that the desire to move is a natural, universal, and reasonable one; and hence that it is not so much a man's desire to move that needs to be justified as any attempt to frustrate the satisfaction of that desire. (Cranston 1973: 31)

A stroll around the neighborhood needn't be tied to any particular goal. The relief felt in escaping a prison sentence does not require further explanation.

The importance of freedom of movement does not in itself demonstrate a right to move across state borders or a right to settle in other countries. The right to move within one's state and to exit one's state are confirmed by many of the major declarations, treatises, and covenants, most prominently Article 13 of the Universal Declaration of Human Rights. But lawmakers have been careful to leave considerable discretion to sovereign states to determine their admission policies. People supporting open borders believe that giving states broad discretion to prevent entry and to settle in their territories is unjust.

The most direct strategy for arguing for a right to immigrate places the burden of proof on those who wish to restrict mobility. States use force to prevent people from immigrating, causing serious harm—at the very least, people are denied access to opportunities that are important to them. As Michael Huemer asks, "Why are we justified in imposing this harm?" (Huemer 2010: 429).

Huemer emphasizes the use of force and the harms this causes. States actively restrict movement across borders through policies that mandate that state employees and their proxies use force to prevent entry and settlement. The EU and Australia intercept boats, forcing people claiming asylum to turn back or diverting them to offshore processing centers (Farrell, Evershed, and Davidson 2016; United Nations Support Mission in Libya 2016). Immigrants, including asylum seekers, are routinely incarcerated around the world (Silverman and Nethery 2015). Increasingly, people who illegally cross borders face criminal penalties (García Hernández 2013).

These examples of force and, indeed, violence are unambiguous. What is less remarked is how force is at the core of institutions, practices, and policies that assign people statuses that systematically disadvantage them. "Immigrant" is a category created by states' legal policy and nation-building efforts (this is why someone who moves thousands of miles within a country is not considered an immigrant). Immigration policy does not simply respond to people who violate state laws through illegal entry, settlement, or employment. Rather, it illegalizes categories of people who then become subject to detention and deportation or find themselves barred from work or separated from their families. States decide who is barred by their laws (e.g., Eritrean refugees forcibly returned to Libya) and who enters (e.g., affluent Americans arriving at European airports). State force is at the core of the creation of these categories of people with curtailed freedoms of movement, opportunity, and family life.

A fundamental moral principle is that the use of force needs justification. This dovetails with the liberal axiom that restrictions on freedom need justification (Carens 1992; Freiman and Hidalgo 2016). Immigration restriction is a *prima facie* rights violation (Huemer 2010: 430). While there may be reasons why states can justly restrict immigration, the burden of proof is on those who favor restriction. Anyone who wants to restrict liberty has the responsibility to justify why the restriction is warranted. This suggests a moral presumption in favor of open borders. Notably, thoughtful critics of open borders generally accept this burden of proof. Their goal is not to dismiss the importance of free movement but to show why it is outweighed by other considerations. While David Miller denies there is a right to immigrate under most circumstances, he admits that people who wish to immigrate deserve that states give their request "due consideration and provide reasons for refusal" (Miller 2016: 37; see also Blake 2013).

Arash Abizadeh connects this liberal obligation to justify immigration restrictions with democracy, arguing that unilaterally imposed immigration controls and democracy are incompatible. Abizadeh connects democracy to coercion, understood to involve either acts (e.g., arresting an immigrant who cannot establish a right to reside in the territory) or threats (e.g., a policy that immigrants who cannot establish their right to reside in the territory will be arrested). Democracy requires that coercion "is actually *justified by and to* the very people over whom it is exercised, in a manner consistent with viewing them as free (autonomous) and equal" (Abizadeh 2008: 41). We cannot claim that a decision is democratic simply because it was made according to a democratic procedure. We also need to ask who was included in making the decision. Democratic principles demanded the expansion of the franchise through women's suffrage, the abolition of slavery, constitutional amendments to lower the voting age, and laws to regularize immigrants' status. Similarly, a regime of border control needs democratic justification from members and from nonmembers subject to state-enforced restrictions.

Abizadeh's argument does not directly support open borders, only that political communities cannot justly unilaterally control their borders.

Nonetheless, the demand that states justify immigration controls to people excluded suggests at the very least much more open borders. Abizadeh concludes that if democratic communities wish to maintain their legitimacy, they must create cosmopolitan democratic institutions with jurisdiction over immigration policy (Abizadeh 2008: 55). In the absence of cosmopolitan democratic institutions, we can use thought experiments to speculate on what justifications people would expect.

One approach is to use a version of John Rawls's original position, a hypothetical social contract meant to simulate a fair and impartial point of view (Rawls 1999). Rawls imagines parties selecting principles of justice from behind a "veil of ignorance." Parties behind the veil of ignorance do not have information about their particular characteristics that might lead to a biased selection of principles of justice. While parties know general facts about society and the world, they do not know anything about their economic or social status, natural assets, interests, life plans, religion, race, ethnicity, or gender. To this list, we can add place of birth. Rawls proposed the original position for a closed society, but other theorists have used it to think about international justice. Joseph Carens asks whether people under the veil of ignorance would choose a right to migrate as a basic liberty:

> In the original position, then, one would insist that the right to migrate be included in the system of basic liberties for the same reasons that one would insist that the right to religious freedom be included: it might prove essential to one's plan of life. (Carens 1987: 258)[2]

There are also indirect strategies for arguing for open borders. As noted earlier, freedom of movement is generally considered to include the right to emigration, even though no state is obliged to accept immigrants. Liberal orthodoxy holds that restrictions on emigration are morally deplorable, proper to the feudal or mercantilist eras or autocratic regimes (Dowty 1987). In practice, this orthodoxy simplifies the relationship between autocracy and emigration. Autocracies often have good reasons to restrict emigration, but they sometimes encourage it to stabilize their regimes and to attract investment and remittances (Miller and Peters 2018). Nonetheless, emigration can also serve as a form of political protest and, in the long run, a cause of democratization (Hirschman 1978: 102).

Liberal orthodoxy upholds a right to emigrate, but simultaneously maintains a corresponding right to restrict immigration (Cole 2000: 44). This creates a problematic asymmetry: many people cannot successfully emigrate, because no country is willing to open its doors. As Ann Dummett points out, "Logically, it is an absurdity to assert a right of emigration without a complementary right of immigration unless there exist in fact (as in the mid-nineteenth century) a number of states which permit free entry" (Dummett 1992: 173).

The logical objection does not imply a right to migrate anywhere in any circumstances (Miller 2016; Wellman and Cole 2011). Freedom of emigration could be theoretically realized if there were at least one place where one could go. That granted, we should be careful not to give too much weight to theoretical possibilities. Meaningful freedom of emigration would mean possessing at least one good place to go. Many people around the world do not in fact have meaningful access to the right to emigrate precisely because they are not able to immigrate anywhere. Legal travel today requires access to passports and visas, which are not in practice available to much of the world's population. This is starkest for those immobilized in refugee camps (Agier 2008) and for stateless people (Bloom, Tonkiss, and Cole 2017). But desperately poor people around the world face often insurmountable barriers to acquiring documents that would allow them to travel.

The real force of the comparison between freedom of movement within states and the corresponding lack of freedom to move across state borders is not logical but moral. The reasons for extensive freedom of movement within states and across states are the same. Joseph Carens begins with the right to internal freedom of movement and observes that the reasons for wanting to move within one's state—employment, family, education, cultural opportunities—are the same reasons one might want to move between states (Carens 2013: 239; see also Oberman 2016). If we hold that extensive freedom of movement is a basic right, it is surprisingly difficult to explain why we shouldn't also endorse freedom of movement between state territories.

COUNTERARGUMENTS

There are three strategies for rejecting the freedom to immigrate. The most audacious response to the claim that there is a *prima facie* right to immigrate is to counter that immigration controls are not coercive. A second strategy is to show that the justification for the right to move and settle is not as broad as claimed, even domestically. Restrictions on mobility and settlement, at least when people have adequate mobility and live in decent homes, are not basic rights violations; instead, they simply frustrate people's attempts to fulfill their preferences. A third strategy is to grant a *prima facie* right to immigrate but show that other rights override it. For example, states' right to self-determination, communities' right to shape their culture, or governments' obligations to prioritize the economic well-being of their citizens might outweigh rights to immigrate. I address the first two strategies here.

David Miller has adopted the first strategy, arguing that immigration controls are not coercive. Under Miller's understanding, coercion occurs when "P forces Q to undertake some relatively specific course of action by communicating an intention to cause bad consequences if that action is not performed" (Miller 2010: 114). Miller gives a paradigmatic example of a mugger who forces someone at knife point to withdraw money from an automatic teller. He proposes a distinction "between *coercion* and *prevention*, where coercion involves forcing a person *to do* some relatively specific thing, and preventing involves forcing a person *not to do* some relatively specific thing while leaving other options open" (Miller 2010: 114). Coercion and prevention are not precise concepts but rather occupy a spectrum in which the progressive removal of alternative options moves prevention closer to coercion.

Miller's strategy is unpromising, echoing Hayek's attempt to deny that impartially applied laws are coercive when their violation is avoidable (Abizadeh 2010: 124; cf. Hayek 1960: 133–47).[3] Miller claims that people are not coerced when they can avoid the threat of preventative laws by not performing the prohibited action. But the mere fact that we are able to avoid the consequences of a coercive threat does not make the threat any less coercive. Laws are coercive precisely because there is a credible threat that the state will deploy force if they are violated. If we followed Miller, we would be forced to conclude that many, if not most, state laws are not coercive and therefore do not require democratic justification (Abizadeh 2010: 122). Border controls are credible precisely because violating them carries the possibility of being subjected to coercive acts. A "preventative" border control not backed by the threat of actual coercion is a mere request that people refrain from entering without permission. Coercive acts are at the core of border controls.

Even if border controls were deemed "preventative" rather than "coercive" (and thus less objectionable), their actual enforcement involves specific acts of coercion. Miller urges us to ignore these specific coercive acts that include "people being bundled on aeroplanes to take them back to their country of origin, or small boats being turned around on the high seas and forced back to their point of departure" and "putting somebody into handcuffs and frog-marching them on to a plane bound for Tehran" (Miller 2010: 112). In his view, it is not the case that "border controls themselves—the act of preventing somebody from entering a specific territory without authorisation—are coercive in the same sense" (Miller 2010: 112).

It may very well be that these specific examples of physical force are coercive in a different sense than restrictive immigration laws that people obey only because of the threat of reprisals. Coercion can be more or less visible, more or less invasive, and more or less morally problematic; this does not change the fact that it is coercion. Furthermore, Miller's decision to not focus on the examples that are coercive obfuscates the violence inherent in immigration enforcement (Sager 2017). Miller's philosophical apparatus allows him to deflect attention from the practices of immigration enforcement. Indeed, the abstract language of rights and utility in political philosophy and applied ethics too often absolves theorists from grappling with the incarceration, deportation, and physical and sexual violence that migrants suffer every day as a result of regimes of migration control.

Even if there is no broad, morally significant distinction between coercion and prevention, Miller has a more compelling claim for why restrictive immigration policies may be less problematic than often thought. The force of his argument turns around the claim that many migrants still retain an adequate set of options in their country of origin even if they are denied entry (Miller 2016: 52; see also Pevnick 2011). In other words, coercion is often justified because it does not sufficiently interfere with would-be immigrants' freedom.

The claim that immigrants retain adequate options is often coupled with the observation that freedom of movement is not absolute. James Griffin denies not only that there is a human right to live anywhere in the world but also that we have a human right to live anywhere we want within a country. As long as people receive sufficient resources for a decent life, their human rights have been met. Though Griffin acknowledges that freedom of residence "should be restricted only for the strongest of reasons" (Griffin 2001: 10), the mere fact that violating our preference to live where we want affects our quality of life does not entail a human rights violation.

Griffin is concerned about the proliferation of human rights. To illustrate why he does not think freedom of movement counts as a human right, Griffin imagines a fictionalized Brazil in which a pair of architects have planned a new capital "Brasilia" inland to help ease population pressure on the coast. After this city is built, the government welcomes a group of new citizens to Brazil but informs them that they will have to settle in the interior of the country. The interior has similar amenities to the coast, along with a reasonable choice of places to live. The government even provides a free shuttle from Brasilia to Rio de Janeiro and São Paulo so people can visit the coast. Griffin acknowledges that the immigrants may prefer to live on the coast but that there is "no human right to the greatest possible satisfaction of one's preferences" (Griffin 2001: 11).

It is helpful to see where Griffin's example goes wrong. Its plausibility rests on the assumption that as long as people have a reasonable range of choices to realize their ends, they have no reason to complain of a human rights violation: "If one is denied a choice between two options that offer equal prospects of a worthwhile life, then it is hard to see any case for claiming a violation of a human right" (Griffin 2001: 11). Though the argument from adequate options often seems to directly address the question of whether borders should be open, it shifts the question from negative to positive duties (Hidalgo 2012: 10). What is problematic about the government's policy is not that it is failing to fulfill a positive duty to provide people obliged to live in Brasilia with the "greatest possible satisfaction of one's preferences"; rather, it is that the government is violating a negative duty not to use force to prevent people from living in a particular place. What violates people's rights is not the fact that governments are failing to help them realize all of their preferences but rather that governments are *preventing* them from doing so. Moreover, they are prevented from doing so because they are immigrants.

The "adequate options" defense of border controls also misrepresents the open-borders position. Open-borders advocates do not hold that human right to freedom of movement entails that people be allowed to take up residence *anywhere* they want. Even within the state, freedom of movement may be restricted. For example, Article 12 of the African Charter on Human and Peoples' Rights cites reasons of "national security, law and order, public health or morality." The American Convention on Human Rights (Article 22) concurs, restricting movement to "prevent crime or to protect national security, public safety, public order, public morals, public health, or the rights or freedoms of others." These range from grave dangers—for example, national security and public safety—to overly broad appeals to "public interest" and "morality." Under normal circumstances, we are not free to move into our neighbor's spare bedroom or backyard. We are compelled to obey city and state ordinances or to purchase permits to visit National Parks. What is different about migration regimes—and in Griffin's fictional Brasilia scenario—is that other mobility restrictions are justified to the population as a whole which (at least in theory) enjoys political representation and other means of contesting injustice.

There are further problems with Griffin's argument. First, we should be very cautious with fictional examples that invoke overpopulation or environmental degradation (I address these types of objections to freedom of immigration in detail in chapter 5). These scenarios are usually unhelpful for thinking seriously about the ethics of human mobility. They invoke extreme circumstances that may allow restrictions on freedom not only for immigrants but also for settled populations—restrictions that would be repugnant under normal circumstances.

Second, Griffin assumes that immigrants have no connections to communities in Brazil. They are represented as outsiders with very different circumstances compared to long-standing residents. He writes: "But the citizens on the seaboard are reluctant to move, and the government is reluctant to force them because forced removal would be likely to break up families and friendships, upset settled expectations, and so on" (Griffin 2001: 10). There are two problematic assumptions here. First, just as we should be cautious about scenarios that presuppose a need for population control, the allusion to forced removal is a red herring. No reasonable immigration policy would allow for the forced removal of settled populations. This would not be immigration but rather colonialism. Second, Griffin assumes that immigrants do not have families and friends, ignoring that even people forced to emigrate do not do so randomly: rather, they follow social networks of family, friends, and community members to particular places.

Griffin's fictional example is institutionalized in Europe's Dublin Regulations that force refugees to asylum in the country of first arrival.[4] This prevents many people from uniting with family already in Europe. These policies are also inefficient, preventing refugees from traveling to countries where they have social networks, language skills, and job opportunities. We can hardly tell a mother separated from her children in England that her freedom has not been curtailed because she can seek asylum in France. Griffin's example and the Dublin Regulation initially appear reasonable because of how methodological nationalism misrepresents immigrants and effaces transnational connections (Sager 2016a). Representing states as isolated containers inhabited by settled national communities ignores, however, the many ways in which people's lives take place in spaces that cross national borders.

Attempts to deny the coercive nature of immigration controls are implausible. Nor does the retort that would-be immigrants have adequate options dissolve the *prima facie* claim that people have a right to immigrate. Rather, the most promising strategy for rejecting freedom of immigration is to accept that there is a *prima facie* right to immigrate, but that is outweighed by other significant rights and liberties. I will address these objections in detail in chapters 5 and 6. Chapter 3 turns to how immigration restrictions play a central role in promulgating inequalities. This provides further compelling reasons for opening borders.

NOTES

1. I leave aside readings of liberalism that see its history and ideals as far more complex and in many cases complicit in justifying colonialism, empire, slavery, and racism (Losurdo 2011; Mignolo 2011). Under these readings, the illiberal treatment of foreigners is not a failure of liberalism but an expected implication of its ideology. Mainstream political philosophers are for the most part confident that they can rescue liberal ideals for the problematic history of the tradition. I am less confident about this.

2. For discussions of Rawlsian approaches, also see Benhabib (2004) and Bertram (2018: 56–60).

3. A strategy that Miller himself roundly rejects in earlier work (Abizadeh 2010: 15)!

4. Regulation (EU) No. 604/2013 of the European Parliament and of the Council of June 26, 2013, available at https://eur-lex.europa.eu/legal-content/EN/TXT/?uri=CELEX:32013R0604.

Chapter 3

Open Borders and
Distributive Justice

Emma worked for the government in the Philippines in child malnourishment policy and education. It didn't pay enough to support her nine children, so she left them in the Philippines with her husband and two caregivers, applied for a tourist visa, and followed her sister to New York. Like many highly educated immigrant workers, Emma was unable to find employment commensurable to her qualifications and work experience in New York. Nonetheless, her first permanent job as a live-in caretaker for two girls paid US$375 a week; back home, she received the equivalent of US$50. Every week she sent her salary home to her family, only keeping her US$20 weekly allowance for herself. For the next decade, she supported her family and her children's education from abroad, communicating by phone and Facebook (Aviv 2016).

Emma's story illustrates the inequalities that propel millions of people to seek work abroad every year, often under adverse conditions. More than 10 million people from the Philippines alone work overseas. In Emma's case, moving to New York allowed her to increase her wages sevenfold, despite moving from a professional job into care work. Her illegalized status limited her ability to use her education and language skills to seek better remunerated work. Much of the low-paid, necessary labor around the world is possible only through immigration policies that provide a vulnerable, exploitable workforce.

So far I have argued that the right to freedom of movement supports open borders. A commitment to distributive justice also leads us to oppose border controls. Coercive border controls not only restrict freedom, but they also drastically lower well-being. Restrictions on the freedom to migrate uphold a global distributive regime in which life chances are determined by place of birth. The next section sets out compelling economic arguments that border controls harm individuals and reduce efficiency.

State border controls also maintain inequities within countries, creating exploitable, illegalized, and temporary workers. These inequities clash with a commitment to moral equality and with the view that people's choices, not their place of birth, should determine their prospects. Furthermore, immigration restrictions produce inequality between and within countries in morally problematic ways. The rest of the chapter defends the position that the economic injustice of border controls goes beyond economic harms and efficiency losses. Border controls are a mechanism for imposing categorical inequalities across ethnic and racial lines, often through mechanisms that uphold white supremacy.

TRILLION DOLLAR BILLS ON THE SIDEWALK

An economist and a physicist come across a $100 bill on the sidewalk. The physicist observes, "Look, there's a $100 bill!" The economist replies, "That's absurd. Somebody would have already picked it up." The joke pokes fun at economic models that presuppose efficient markets that automatically allocate resources to where they are most valued. In these models, $100 bills on the sidewalk do not exist.

In reality, markets are inefficient, distorted by quotas and tariffs, monopolies and monopsonies, and incomplete and asymmetrical information. Immigration controls are among the most significant market distortions. A substantial portion of workers' productivity results not from their human capital but rather from their location (Milanovic 2013: 204). Workers from lower-wage countries could move to countries where they would receive higher wages and produce more value if it were not for restrictive immigration policies. This is akin to leaving trillion dollar bills on the sidewalk (Clemens 2011).

Increased liberalization of human mobility would lead to economic gain by increasing efficiency.[1] Though estimates vary, even a modest increase in labor mobility would lead to billions of dollars in efficiency gains. Lant Pritchett cites a 2005 World Bank study that estimates a $300 billion gain from a 3 percent rise in labor mobility (Pritchett 2006; see also, World Bank 2005 and Martin 2005). Ana María Iregui places the efficiency gains at more than 50 percent of the world gross domestic product (Iregui 2005). Jonathon W. Moses and Bjorn Letnes have developed a model which suggests that free mobility could lead to an efficiency gain of US$3.4 trillion (2005; cf. Chang 2007).

A substantial portion of these efficiency gains goes directly to workers who migrate from poorer regions. Michael Clemens, Claudio Montenegro, and Lant Pritchett compare US immigrant workers and workers in forty-two developing countries to estimate what they call the "place premium"—the wage gap determined solely by location. They conclude that the average price equivalent of migration barriers exceeds $13,700 per worker per year (Clemens, Montenegro, and Pritchett 2019).

A more liberal migration regime could lead not only to greater efficiency but also to greater equality between regions. In theory, open borders would lead to rising wages in the country of emigration and falling wages in the country of immigration, eventually reaching an equilibrium at which immigration would halt. Timothy J. Hatton and Jeffrey G. Williamson, in their economic history of the mass migrations from Europe to the New World between 1850 and 1914, conclude that European mass emigration raised real wages and lowered unemployment in Europe as well as slowed the pace of real wage growth in countries of emigration, leading to economic convergence (Hatton and Williamson 1998). John Kennan calculates that open borders could more than double the income level in less-developed countries with only a small decrease in real wages in developed countries, leading to welfare gains of more than $10,000 a year for randomly chosen developing-country workers (*including* those who do not migrate) (Kennan 2013).

The effects of migration resonate beyond the real wage gains of migrants. Migration also leads to remittances, cross-border skill transfer, circular migration, technological bridges, and other factors known to spur economic development. Kieran Oberman usefully surveys the literature on remittances and concludes that they benefit the people who receive them by lowering infant mortality and by increasing literacy and school attendance; they are also used for consumption and investment in education, agriculture, and business, benefiting people in the surrounding community who do not directly receive remittances (Oberman 2015: 243). John Kenneth Galbraith's words continue to resonate:

> Migration is the oldest action against poverty. It selects those who most want help. It is good for the country to which they go; it helps break the equilibrium of poverty in the country from which they come. What is the perversity in the human soul that causes people to resist so obvious a good? (Galbraith 1979; cited in Legrain 2007: 1)

BIRTHRIGHT PRIVILEGE AND CATEGORICAL INEQUALITIES

The perversity of the human soul that leads people to oppose migration is uglier than what Galbraith suggests. We would have reason to endorse open borders if their only benefit were global efficiency gains. We would have still more reason to endorse them if they also promoted development and equality. But border controls not only prevent people from escaping poverty and ameliorating inequalities, but they also play a central role in causing them. Moreover, the motivations justifying border controls are mired in racist legacies and ideas that deny immigrants equal rights and respect.

Morally desirable outcomes are important, but they are not all that matter. We also care how they are achieved. Too often debates about global justice ignore the causes of inequality or place the blame on the poor choices of governments or citizens. For example, some theorists attempt to deflect demands to open borders by denying that egalitarian obligations extend to people outside of the political community. While authors such as Michael Blake and David Miller agree that there may be obligations to ensure that people outside of state or national communities enjoy sufficient resources or basic rights, but this does not mean that they are entitled to equality (Blake 2013a, 2014; Miller 2016). The implication is that distributive justice may support *more* open borders, but the right to migrate should not extend to would-be immigrants who can have decent lives in their country of origins.

This way of viewing global inequality presupposes a level playing field in which countries developed independently, ignoring how colonialism and imperialism still resonate, contributing to inequality and to poverty (Mongia 2018). The methodological nationalist tendency to imagine countries as isolated containers has allowed theorists to ignore the profound, ongoing interconnections between regions. It permits them to overlook how privileged groups today continue to cause inequalities through national and international policies. This is a serious omission for a moral analysis of poverty and inequality, allowing culpable parties to evade moral responsibility by portraying themselves as bystanders.

Border controls are among the most significant causes of global inequalities. Restricting immigration not only maintains cross-border inequalities, but it also causes them. Joseph Carens called citizenship in Western states "the modern equivalent of feudal privilege—an inherited status that greatly enhances one's life's chances" (Carens 1987: 252). Borders concentrate wealth in particular regions by excluding people, actively distributing benefits and burdens in ways that favor the residents of the developed world (admittedly favoring some of these residents more than others). Meanwhile, these developed state residents employ violence to keep the global poor at home.

Charles Tilly and Douglas Massey's analysis of "categorical inequalities" helps us understand the processes that maintain birthright privileges. Tilly and Massey research the mechanisms that cause stratification in which people are grouped into social categories such as race, gender, or class, causing their unequal access to scarce resources. Often categories become an unquestioned part of the social fabric, leading many people to overlook them and to attribute inequalities to individual differences. Massey identifies two main mechanisms that combine to explain stratification: first, people are allocated to social categories; second, institutional practices mobilize these categories so that resources are allocated to groups (Massey 2007: 5–6).

Opportunity hoarding and exploitation are two mechanisms for generating and perpetuating inequality (Massey 2007: 6–7; see also Tilly 1999). Opportunity hoarding restricts access to scarce resources by excluding stratified groups. Exploitation occurs when one group expropriates resources produced by another group. The category of "immigrant" enables both opportunity hoarding and exploitation. We can see this through an analysis of the category itself, as well as through analysis of how the social kind of "immigrant" is constructed. Immigrant is a state category that designates people excluded from full membership rights. Immigrants, by definition, have fewer legal rights and privileges than citizens. Even privileged permanent residents who enjoy most of the rights of citizens generally lack voting rights and are vulnerable to deportation.

States marshal the categories of immigrant and citizen to allocate resources by providing access to opportunities. They prevent would-be immigrants from entering their territories and thus accessing territorial-based legal and economic systems. Within countries, people categorized as immigrants find themselves marginalized and racialized because of their legal and social categorizations. They are legally excluded from labor markets or included with fewer rights and opportunities. For example, they are often allowed only to work for particular employers or in particular sectors. Their credentials and skills are also often ignored or discounted, affecting their ability to compete. They are also stereotyped and subject to discrimination.

We cannot evaluate the moral status of allocating opportunities through the category of immigrant without examining the techniques and processes that create and reify it. The category of immigrant only emerges in a political system of nation-states dominated by the idea of universal citizenship, supported by identity documents such as passports and visas (Torpey 2000). The existence of immigrants depends on ongoing bureaucratic, social, and ideological processes that maintain their unequal status. It ultimately rests on states' willingness to reify the category by employing police to exclude, round up, detain, and deport people. Moreover, the social and legal classifications that identify people as immigrants are often racialized. David Scott FitzGerald and David Cook-Martín have analyzed racist policies in the Americas, showing how twenty-two countries in the Western hemisphere selected immigrants by ethnicity, either through negative discrimination against some groups (e.g., through bans, quotas, or entry taxes) or through positive preferences (e.g., assisted passage, free land, or exemptions from requirements enforced against other groups) (FitzGerald and Cook-Martín 2014: 33). Explicit ethnic discrimination disappeared from these countries' immigration and nationality laws by 2010, but their legacy reverberates today.

Migration history helps elucidate the logic of immigration policy and the categories that it creates and employs. In the United States, both scholarship and popular imagination have treated the history of slavery, reconstruction, and Jim Crow laws as distinct from immigration. Recent American myth presents the country as a "nation of immigrants," a "melting pot" in which Europeans blended their past with their new American identity (Magee 2009: 27). This fiction came to prominence during the Cold War, with John F. Kennedy's 1958 publication, *A Nation of Immigrants* (Gabaccia 2010: 23). The myth of the melting pot ignores the hostility toward many European immigrant groups at the time. Moreover, it is deeply Eurocentric, effacing the racist treatment of Asian, African, and Middle Eastern immigrants and the virtual prohibition of non-European immigration for much of the twentieth century (Hing 2009: 39). It also evades troubling similiarities between the treatment of immigrant and slavery and the oppression and the exclusion of Native Americans. (Native Americans were not US citizens until the passage of the Indian Citizenship Act of 1924 and remained excluded from the franchise by states until 1962 when New Mexico finally enfranchised them.) As Mae M. Ngai observes:

> The theme of universal inclusion and citizenship could be read back onto the eighteenth and nineteenth centuries only by bracketing the conquest of Native Americans, slavery, southwestern annexation, Asiatic exclusion, Jim Crow, and the acquisition of unincorporated territories (colonies). (Ngai 2004: xxiv)

Africans brought to the continent through the transatlantic slave trade have for the most part been studied independently from immigration history. Rhonda Magee proposes viewing chattel slavery as "among very many other things, *a compulsory form of immigration, the protection and regulation of which, under federal and state law, was our nation's first system of 'immigration law'*" (Magee 2009: 4). She suggests that we should acknowledge that slavery was a system of human trafficking and see the federal laws that protected slavery as a form of immigration law (19) "aimed at fulfilling the need for a controllable labour population in the colonies, and then in the states, at an artificial low economic cost" (Magee 2009: 5). In her analysis, slavery founded a racially segmented labor-based immigration system (Magee 2009; also see Hing 2009: 19). She finds a parallel in how immigrants are socially and culturally constructed as "non-citizens" and "quasi-citizens" (Magee 2009: 25), and how slavery anticipates other forms of racially segmented labor-based immigration.

This was partly achieved through law. Laws such as the Nationality Act of 1790 "limited naturalization to 'free white persons'" (Hing 2009). Notorious

˙cases in immigration law such as *Chae Chan Ping*,[2] *Ekiu*,[3] and *Fong Yue Ting*[4] laid the foundation for the plenary power doctrine, granting the federal government broad, discretionary power over the admission and deportation of noncitizens (Mendoza 2016a: 2–5). *Takao Ozawa v. United States* (1922) and *United States v. Bhagat Singh Thind* (1923) established that, for the purposes of US law, Japanese and Indian people were not white (Mendoza 2016b: 211–13).

Racism and xenophobia have played a major role in establishing categories that enable the exclusion and exploitation of groups. Jonathon Moses draws an analogy between South Africa under apartheid and international border controls:

> Black South Africans needed official permission to travel and work anywhere within the country. Specific permits were required to look for jobs, to take jobs, and then to change jobs. The requirement to register, and to produce the dreaded *dompas* (an internal passport), was both cumbersome and humiliating. (Moses 2006: 85)

While many people in countries like the United States recoil at the comparison of their immigration policies with South African apartheid, the analogy is robust. In particular, the construction of whiteness has played a central part in the ability to exclude (Jacobson 2002). Labeling groups as "non-white" allows for their segregation, exploitation, and expulsion (Mendoza 2016b). In the cases of the Japanese, their "white" status was removed through a combination of legislation, court decisions, and xenophobic social movements, culminating in the Supreme Court decision *Korematsu v. United States* (1944) that upheld the constitutionality of President Roosevelt's order to confine Japanese Americans to internment camps.

Plenary power and racialized enforcement practices combined to create docile workers. This is explicit in the history of immigration from Mexico. In June 1954, the US Border Patrol announced "Operation Wetback," a continuation of its policy of apprehending and deporting unsanctioned Mexican immigrants since the mid-1940s (Hernández 2010). With the help of law enforcement in California and Arizona, the Border Patrol raided neighborhoods and trains, as well as recruited police to detain suspected unauthorized immigrants on vagrancy charges and turn them over for deportation (Calavita 1992: 54). Hundreds of thousands of Mexican migrants were deported from 1953 to 1955 (Ngai 2004: 156–7). Kitty Calavita notes the "widespread reports of abuses by the Border Patrol and charges that legal residents and in some cases American citizens had been deported, harassed and/or beaten" (Calavita 1992: 54). Operation Wetback's main function was to not eliminate Mexican immigration. Rather, it was to channel workers into the Bracero Program. Many US employers preferred not to use the Bracero Program, which mandated a minimum wage and sanitary living conditions, so they refused to cooperate with the Border Patrol (Hernandez 2017). Many deported workers returned as Bracero Program recruits.

Operation Wetback is the best-known example of mass deportation of people of Mexican heritage, perhaps because of its racist moniker. Less notorious and even more ignominious is the "repatriation" of persons of Mexican ancestry from the United States in the 1930s—in which approximately 60 percent of those removed were American citizens (Johnson 2005: 104; also see Balderrama and Rodriguez 2006). The "repatriation" violated the legal rights of hundreds of thousands of people who were deported, as well as "stopped, interrogated, and detained but not removed from the country" (Johnson 2005: 105). Kevin Johnson describes the impact of these mass deportations as terrorizing and traumatizing the Mexican American community (Johnson 2005: 105).

These mass deportations should be understood as part of an ongoing process in which the United States employs legal and political mechanisms to maintain categorical inequalities with the Hispanic/Latinx population. Even with the repeal of overtly racist policies and laws with the 1965 Immigration and Nationality Act, immigration policy continues to disproportionately affect the Mexican community. The Act imposed a cap of 20,000 persons-per-year on every country in the world, regardless of their current levels of immigration. Though facially nondiscriminatory, this led to hundreds of thousands of Mexicans who previously enjoyed the right to be in the country losing their legal status (FitzGerald and Cook-Martín 2014: 132). Another way of describing this process is that the state illegalized hundreds of thousands of Mexicans.

The process of illegalization portrays people as outside of the community. Bill Ong Hing discusses how scapegoating of immigrants in the media and the political sphere has led to their demonization and dehumanization (Hing 2009; see also Haslam and Stratemeyer 2016). Immigrants are simultaneously accused of taking jobs and of draining public benefits, as well as of criminal activity. During the electoral campaign, presidential candidate Donald Trump referred to the US-born children of immigrants as "anchor babies," called Mexican immigrants rapists and killers (though he admitted that some are "good people"), and characterized Muslims as "Trojan horses." This rhetoric was not unique to Trump. Republican candidate Ben Carson referred to Syrian refugees as "rabid dogs," and Republican candidate Ted Cruz called for law enforcement to patrol Muslim neighborhoods after terrorist attacks in Brussels (Kteily and Bruneau 2017: 87).

After Trump's election, we witnessed the Executive Order "Protecting the Nation from Foreign Terrorist Entry"—dubbed by many the "Muslim ban"—in its chaotic first version, then again in substantially similar revised versions, ultimately upheld by the Supreme Court (Chishti, Pierce, and Plata 2018). President Trump also lamented refugee protections for immigrants who come from "shithole countries"—he included Haiti, El Salvador, and the African continent in this category—suggesting instead bringing immigrants from countries like Norway (Dawsey 2018). His administration created VOICE—Victims of Immigration Crime Engagement office—which has been charged with registering criminal offenses by immigrants, a cynical measure designed to categorize immigrants as criminals (Kopan 2017). The Trump administration has coupled it with a publication of all detention requests turned down by local jails, advertised as necessary to "better inform the public regarding the public safety threats associated with sanctuary jurisdictions" (Gomez 2017). These threats are not supported by evidence (Landgrave and Nowrasteh 2019). In practice, it aims to shame Sanctuary Cities that choose to not use resources from local law enforcement to enforce federal immigration law.

Though the racism of the Trump administration is thinly disguised, immigration discussions are often carried out in seeming race-neutral terms such as "illegal" or "criminal" aliens, alleging that unauthorized migration is a question of the rule of law, unconnected to racism (Hing 2009: 41). Anti-immigrant organizations such as The Federation for American Immigration Reform and the Center for Immigration Studies have effectively mobilized this language, finding a voice in mainstream media. They are careful to stress in their outreach to the media and broader community that they are not against legal immigrants already present in the country. Rather, they wish to restrict the number of new immigrants admitted and to remove "illegal immigrants."

Though these groups claim to object to immigrants not because of what they are but because of their illegal actions, this tactic does not stand up to scrutiny. As Josiah Heyman points out, illegal status is a legal and social construction: people are made illegal by political decisions that classify them as outside of the social and political communities (Heyman 2011). A sincere opposition to illegal entry or presence would also ask why the laws governing migration are in place. If *illegality* were the root of the problem, critics would be open to changing laws, so people would be able to regularize their status.

Instead, illegalization is a central mechanism for imposing categorical inequalities on groups of immigrants, which in turn contributes to their dehumanization. As Kevin Johnson notes, "Illegal alien is a pejorative term that implies criminality, thereby suggesting that the persons who fall in this category deserve punishment, not legal protection" (Johnson 1996–1997: 276). The increasingly broad range of deportable offenses supports claims that immigrants are criminals, undermining sympathy and justifying deportation (Aja and Marchevsky 2017; García Hernández 2013; Stumpf 2006). Jennifer

Chacón has detailed a shift over the past twenty years in which the US government has dramatically expanded federal criminal sanctions to immigration law, as well as involved state and local law enforcement in policing low-level criminal offenses that can result in deportation (Chacón 2012). She argues that this constitutes overcriminalization, resulting in the excessive punishment for immigration offenses:

> By imposing criminal law solutions on what is (and has always been) primarily an issue of labour migration flow, legislatures have not only failed to address the central dynamics that drive migration, but have also created a series of undesirable and expensive by-products. (Chacón 2012: 649)

These by-products include racial profiling. Immigration policies interact with structural racism. Many immigrants find themselves disadvantaged in segregated neighborhoods. The criminal justice system compounds the harm through laws that allow the deportation of permanent residents. Hing argues that

> the structure of immigration laws has institutionalized a set of values that dehumanize, demonize, and criminalize immigrants of color. The result is that these victims stop being Mexicans, Latinos, or Chinese and become "illegal immigrants." (Hing 2009:3)

Anti-immigration rhetoric in the United States conceives immigrants as Mexican, Muslim, or Chinese, rather than as Canadian or Irish (Wang, Hurt, and Domonoske 2017). The popular imagination does not connect the category of "illegal immigrant" primarily to a legal status (e.g., it is not on par with the category of "traffic law violators" or "shoplifters") but rather is mingled with racial and ethnic stereotypes. Kevin Johnson quotes Gerald Neuman:

> The discourse of legal [immigration] status permits coded discussion in which listeners will understand that reference is being made, *not to aliens in the abstract, but to the particular foreign group that is the principal focus of current hostility.* (Johnson 1996–1997: 281, citing Neuman 1994–1995: 1429)

Racial stigmatization is compounded by state measures to deny immigrants employment, education, and statutory entitlements such as food stamps or medical services and threatens to turn immigrants into "pariahs." Owen Fiss writes:

> The subjugation produced by the laws imposing social disabilities on immigrants is, however, of another character, for what is entailed is not simply drawing a distinction among people, but rather creating a different kind of social structure altogether: it entails a further stratification or degradation of the very

poor, or in Justice Brennan's words, "raises the spectre of a permanent caste." (Fiss 1998)

I have focused on the United States, but similar points can be made elsewhere. Around the world, migrants are recruited with temporary status and limited rights, precisely so they can serve as a cheap, disposable workforce. This was true of the British Empire's use of indentured labor and "free" migration of colonial subjects after the abolition of slavery (Mongia 2018). It is also true of Western Europe's employment of "guest workers," often from former colonies, to rebuild the European economy after World War II. Similar points can be made of temporary laborers and caregivers in the Arab states or in Hong Kong and Singapore or for seasonal workers brought to Canada (Basok 2009). In fact, temporary labor programs around the world are built on unequal rights.

The role of the modern state as the primary guarantor of rights means that people who do not enjoy full membership rights frequently find their human rights unprotected (Kingston 2019). Immigrants are by definition people who do not enjoy the full panoply of legal rights. This makes them vulnerable to exploitation and exclusion from opportunities. None of this is accidental; it is how the category of immigrant functions.

Let me take stock. People are assigned by birth to countries with starkly unequal opportunities. Immigration policies prevent much of the world's population from legally seeking better opportunities abroad. These policies should not be understood as allowing inequality but as producing it. People from around the world could benefit by immigrating but cannot because of policies that uphold the privilege of people with the good fortune to be born in richer regions. Furthermore, people categorized as immigrants within states are vulnerable to exploitation and have less access to opportunities because of their immigrant status. Categorical inequalities lead to enormous inequalities between states because less well-off people are prevented from immigrating; they also play a major role within states, supporting the exploitation of immigrants with precarious legal status and limited access to civil and labor rights. As Nicholas De Genova observes, "The category of 'illegal alien' is a profoundly useful and profitable one that effectively serves to create and sustain a legally vulnerable—and hence, relatively tractable and thus 'cheap'—reserve of labor" (De Genova 2002: 440). A similar logic applies to temporary labor programs. A commitment to distributive justice demands that we open borders because of their effects on global inefficiency and equality and because inequalities are actively produced by immigration policies, which construct people born elsewhere as outside of the community, often by racializing and dehumanizing them.

OBJECTIONS

Political philosophers have expressed skepticism about arguments for open borders based on the demands of distributive justice (Brock 2009; Miller 2005). Some of this skepticism is based on views about the economics of immigration. First, some theorists claim that immigration harms so-called low-skilled domestic workers that states have a moral duty to prioritize (Macedo 2018).[5] Second, there is the claim that emigration, particularly of skilled workers, causes "brain drain," shifting human capital from low-wage regions to high-wage regions with disastrous effects for long-term development and the well-being of those left behind. Alternatively, critics can accept the economic case but argue that there are alternative ways of reaching the same objectives without allowing a significant rise in immigration. One proposal is that it is possible to substitute development aid for immigration. On this account, states that have obligations of international or global distributive justice can elect to meet them by providing aid, rather than by allowing immigration.

Another prominent alternative both in political philosophy and policy circles is to advocate for expanding temporary migration programs. Advocates for these programs suggest that many of the goals of distributive justice can be achieved by creating legal avenues for people to come and work with strict time limits to avoid permanent settlement. Temporary migration programs fall short of open borders by imposing selection criteria and numerical caps on potential immigrants and by assigning temporary workers fewer rights than citizens.

DOES DISTRIBUTIVE JUSTICE SUPPORT OPEN BORDERS?

Economic arguments for open borders are compelling if we look at the benefits of immigration to individual migrants or examine the aggregate effects of migration. Nonetheless, the economic costs and benefits of migration are not distributed equally. Even if we agree that migration is beneficial on aggregate, some groups may be adversely affected. Since some theorists believe that distributive justice requires giving priority to compatriots (Miller 2017) or privileging the most disadvantaged (Rawls 1999; Higgins 2013), under some circumstances immigration justice might require restricting immigration.

People invoking distributive justice to restrict immigration often base their account on immigration's alleged effect on local workers. Simple economic models tell us that, in a competitive market, an influx of people competing for the same jobs will lead to lower wages. George Borjas is frequently cited as showing that "low-skilled" immigration to the United States has had a substantial, negative effect on American-born workers. For example, in a 2003 study, Borjas contends that the 11 percent increase in labor supply of immigrant men in 1980 reduced the wages of the average native worker by 3.2 percent (Borjas 2003: 1370).

Though Borjas enjoys significant media attention as a mainstream economist with consistently bleak views on the effects of immigration, his analysis is disputed by many of his peers (Card 2005; Ottaviano and Peri 2012). In an influential economic study, David Card took advantage of the 1980 arrival of 125,000 mostly "low-skilled" immigrants in Miami from Mariel Bay, Cuba, for a natural experiment. Simple models of supply and demand do not adequately account for the effects of immigration. Under these models, the increase in a supply of "low-skilled" immigrants would lead already-present "low-skilled" workers to receive lower wages in the years following 1980. But Card was unable to find evidence of an effect on unemployment or on wage rates of "low-skilled" non-Cuban workers (Card 1990). While we are not certain why Card did not find any effect, one possibility is that the Cubans' occupations complemented, rather than competed, with the occupations of other "low-skilled" workers. It's also possible that employers took advantage of the influx of labor and created new jobs that otherwise would not have existed. Another factor is that immigrants also create demand, generating jobs. A common error in popular views about immigration and jobs is that the supply of jobs is fixed for a static number of open positions, so more workers means more competition; this omits how workers are also consumers, so in many cases more people creates more jobs (Chang 2008).[6]

What about claims that immigrants' use of public benefits exceeds their tax contributions or that they strain public services? Though the effects of immigration vary from place to place depending on government policy, research on its overall fiscal effects suggests that they are largely neutral (Organization for Economic Cooperation and Development 2013; National Academies of Sciences, Engineering, and Medicine 2017). Nonetheless, increases in immigration do not come without burdens that are sometimes unevenly distributed, especially over the short term. Local governments and populations may face immediate costs in education or housing while not receiving some of the benefits accrued at the regional or state level. This is grounds for redistribution, not for restricting immigration.

We should acknowledge these burdens but recognize that immigration is a convenient scapegoat for the challenges of rapid social and economic change. Restricting immigration is rarely an effective policy measure for addressing these changes. Even when some people are adversely affected, the gains from immigration allow for their compensation. As Howard Chang points out, if the well-being of "unskilled" local workers is our concern, progressive taxation and transfer policies are less costly than protectionist immigration policies (Chang 2008: 10). What distributive justice demands is not closing borders but rather economic and social policies that provide vulnerable people with a robust social security net. These measures have the added benefit of not curtailing freedoms of movement and opportunity.

So far I have accepted the normative assumptions of those who wish to restrict immigration because of its alleged effects on native workers. These authors (either implicitly or explicitly) assume that we are justified in giving substantial weight to the interests of people who have already settled. In doing so, they hold that distributive justice can take into account special ties and associations, allowing us to privilege compatriots. Even if we accept that there are grounds to privilege people within our political community, this does not support restricting migration unless we're prepared to heavily or entirely discount the interests of nonmembers. Compare Borjas's contention that the average American worker suffers a 3.2-percent wage decrease to Michael Clemens, Claudio Montenegro, and Lant Pritchett's estimate that many people from many regions can more than quadruple their real wages by immigrating (Clemens, Montenegro, and Pritchett 2019). Sacrificing the huge gains to potential immigrants for the relatively small losses to settled workers goes beyond compatriot priority, suggesting that the interests of people outside of the nation-state count for little or even nothing.

Another common claim is that distributive justice may demand immigration restrictions because "skilled" emigration can have bad effects for those left behind, through "brain drain" (a pejorative term for "the emigration of skilled workers," especially from poorer to richer regions). "Brain drain" is often blamed for hindering development and depriving those left behind of key services, especially in health care (Brock and Blake 2015). The "brain drain" objection is often invoked against current immigration policies of many countries that favor professional immigrants, while providing limited immigration opportunities for workers in three-dimensional (dirty, dangerous, and difficult) jobs. If the emigration of professionals exacerbates inequalities, distributive justice might recommend migration restrictions for these workers.

Though the existence of harmful "brain drain" is often considered established, the empirical evidence is far from conclusive, even in the oft-cited case of emigrating healthcare workers (Clemens 2016; Docquier and Rapoport 2012; Hidalgo 2016). Much of the research on "skilled" emigration faces serious challenges in acquiring reliable data and uses models that have not been rigorously tested against empirical evidence. Even when there is a correlation between emigration and poor outcomes in sending countries, it is difficult to establish that emigration causes these outcomes—in many cases, weak institutions, few opportunities, corruption, and violence may hinder development *and* cause educated people to leave. People invoking "brain drain" as a reason to limit migration often stress the need for educated people to remain to build effective institutions. This assumes opportunities that may not exist. If emigrants had real opportunities to use their education to improve their country's institutions, they would have a significant incentive to stay. Their emigration suggests a dearth of opportunities. It also overlooks the possibility of emigrants' transnational political or economic action to improve conditions in their countries of origin from abroad.

Moreover, research shows that in many cases "skilled" emigration leads to remittances, transnational business connections, and, eventually, returning migrants who use knowledge acquired abroad in the local economy. The opportunity to emigrate may also provide people with an incentive to acquire education, known as "brain gain" (Beine, Docquier, and Rapoport 2008). This research finds an overall rise in education in some regions, since some workers who pursued education with plans of emigrating end up not going abroad.

Finally, "brain drain" is rarely a good justification for migration restrictions (Oberman 2013). We should be cautious about restricting freedom, especially if other measures are available. Too often, the "brain drain" debate treats migration as independent from the policies that regulate it. It emphasizes the potentially harmful effects of emigration without asking about the full range of policies that could ameliorate them. Most immigration-related issues of distributive justice can be addressed by policy measures that do not directly restrict migration but rather shape it for mutual benefit. In fact, undue attention to the economic effects of migration distracts us from more fundamental ways in which our world fails to meet standards of distributive justice (Sager 2014; Sager 2016a). It allows local and national politicians to scapegoat emigrants (and for that matter immigrants) instead of promoting the social and economic rights of their constituencies and reducing corruption that entrenches local elites or multinational corporations. It also diverts attention away from internationally imposed austerity programs and the asymmetrical competition that benefits wealthy countries.

PAYING TO KEEP OUT THE OTHER

Another strategy is to accept the economic case for more open borders but argue that taking in immigrants can be avoided by transferring resources. If the duty to accept immigrants is closely tied to distributive justice, then it might be possible to meet one's duty by transferring resources across borders, rather than by allowing migration. Andrew Altman and Christopher Heath Wellman argue:

> Thus, no matter how substantial their duties of distributive justice, wealthier countries need not open their borders. At most, affluent societies are duty-bound to choose between allowing needy foreigners to enter their society or sending some of their wealth to those less fortunate. (Altman and Wellman 2009; see also Kymlicka 2001: 271)[7]

This sentiment extends beyond academic discussions. One component of the European Commissions' Partnership Framework is increasing development aid to address what the Commission perceives as the root causes of emigration (Siegfried 2016). This proposal comes over ten years after the then president of the European Commission José Manuel Barroso said that "the problem of immigration, the dramatic consequences of which we are witnessing, can only be addressed effectively . . . through an ambitious and coordinated development [plan] to fight its root causes" (cited Haas 2007a: 820),[8]

According to this view, egalitarian concerns can be addressed by transferring resources across borders, rather than by allowing migration. Sound development policies could be substituted for immigration. In fact, since immigration will directly affect only those who migrate, some claim that instead of advocating open borders—which face considerable opposition—people should rather focus on promoting global equality by fostering development. Peter W. Higgins argues for a "Priority of Disadvantage Principle" to govern immigration policies (2013). He holds that the most unjustly disadvantaged people tend not to migrate. Since international travel is still costly, immigrants are often drawn from the middle classes and have better opportunities at home than many of their fellow citizens. Immigrants tend to be young, healthy, ambitious, and better educated than many of their compatriots. During political upheaval or natural disasters, elites with advanced degrees, language skills, and international contacts are often in the best position to migrate.

Higgin's arguments are similar to an account put forward by Thomas Pogge in which egalitarians concerned about global poverty should not devote resources toward opening borders, but rather toward effective programs of poverty eradication (Pogge 1997: 12). In Pogge's view, admitting needy foreigners will hardly make a dent in absolute poverty. Given the scale of poverty, migration would need to be dramatically increased in order to directly ameliorate even extreme poverty—levels that almost certainly would be rejected by the voters of industrial states.

Pogge's either/or dichotomy between immigration and development aid is wrongheaded. We should advocate for both. Immigration plays a necessary role in discharging obligations of distributive justice, but it will not abolish absolute poverty or rid the world of the deep, structural inequalities that divide regions and societies. Migration interacts with economic and political institutions, culture, geography, and many other factors that make its impact complex and sometime opaque. Still, there is good reason to believe that its impact is on the whole positive and that it is possible to design better institutions to bolster these positive effects and to mitigate its harms (Haas 2007b).

Open-borders advocates hold that migration is a major means of addressing poverty but are not committed to the view that the fact that people could migrate to improve their situation means that people should be encouraged, let alone forced, to migrate. Kieran Oberman argues that immigration policy should be a policy of last resort for poverty alleviation (Oberman 2015). This seems to me too strong, since the most appropriate tools and policies for poverty alleviation depend on the context—sometimes migration may be the measure with the lowest cost or the highest chance of success. It may also be the preferred option of the poor. Nonetheless, governments shouldn't renege on the obligation to build institutions and infrastructure simply because people have the possibility of migrating.

In general, we need to understand that the movement of capital and labor across borders are not perfectly substitutable; they complement each other (Cohen 2006: 111–13). They are mutually supporting, creating feedback loops in which migration begets development. In the short run, economic development leads to *more* migration, not less, as we see when large numbers of people migrate from the countryside to the cities in the developing world (Cohen 2006; Haas 2012). Furthermore, remittances, skill transfer, and circular migration may be among the more effective means of boosting development. Any sensible agenda for development must address migration and, very likely, encourage it in some form. There is no neat trade-off between developmental aid and immigration. Rather, immigration is part of any sensible plan for development (Clemens and Postel 2018).

Indeed, in some respects this whole debate is misconceived, mired in the assumptions of methodological nationalism. Using state boundaries as the unit of analysis for measuring development often fails to track improvements in human well-being or flourishing. State-centered models do not treat emigration as part of development. This has paradoxical implications, as Michael Clemens and Lant Pritchett note:

> If a Salvadoran moves from the countryside to San Salvador and gets a factory job that raises her income by 30 percent, this will be recorded as progress. But if that same person moves to Texas, gets an identical factory job, and increased her income fivefold, this does not increase income per capital in El Salvador. . . . Worse, if her wage was above the average in El Salvador, then income per capita goes down.

Moreover, if her new job in Texas pays less than the average US wage, then income per resident in the United States goes down as well. Income per capita could decline in both sending and receiving places because the place-based national-accounts measures exclude the gains to the person who moved. (Clemens and Pritchett 2008: 395–96)

Clemens and Pritchett instead propose "Income per Natural" which measures increases in average income in a way that takes migration into account. Using data on household income for foreign-born populations from the 2000 US census, they first estimate the income per natural in the high-income Organization for Economic Co-operation and Development by country of birth, then generalize the results of their analysis to obtain estimates for the rest of the world. Their analysis shows that migration is a primary source of poverty reduction around the world and that "over a billion people live in countries whose collective income per capita would rise more than 10 percent if considered as income per natural rather than income per resident." (Clemens and Pritchett 2008: 423). If we care primarily about people, not places, migration is a form of development.

TEMPORARY MIGRATION

A final response to distributive justice-based arguments for open borders is that they can be discharged by allowing more temporary labor. According to the International Labour Organization, there were 164 million migrant workers in 2017, 95.7 million men and 68.1 million women (Popova et al. 2018). The majority of these migrants work in Northern, Western, and Southern Europe, North America, and the Arab states. The Arab states hosted 32 million international migrants in 2015, mostly from Asia and Africa. These workers make up the majority of the population in Bahrain, Oman, Qatar, and the United Arab Emirates, performing 95 percent of the construction and domestic work.

Temporary worker programs allow countries to bring in workers to address labor shortages. They vary in the length of time workers can remain, the opportunities to renew visas or to transfer to permanent residence, the ability of workers to leave employers without becoming vulnerable to deportation, the right to bring family, and the access to social programs. Some temporary worker programs such as the *kafala* (sponsorship system) in Qatar require an exit visa for workers to leave and tie workers to a single employer who often confiscates their documents. Others such as Canada's Live-in Caregiver Program (now suspended to new applicants) provide a path to permanent residence. Nonetheless, all temporary worker programs provide migrants with fewer rights than citizens (Lenard and Straehle 2011).

Could temporary worker programs substitute for open borders? In theory, temporary worker programs promote circular migration, providing a win-win-win solution for all parties: receiving countries and their employers win by receiving a flexible, low-wage workforce; sending countries win by receiving remittances, as well as an outlet for surplus labor; and migrants win by gaining access to higher-wage regions. Many immigration advocates suggest that temporary worker programs are an acceptable alternative, especially given the challenge of passing laws allowing more permanent immigration.

Martin Ruhs observes that if employers must give temporary workers the same rights as native workers—including the power to change employers or to move across labor sectors—then they have little reason to recruit foreign workers (Ruhs 2013). Howard Chang calls this "The Immigration Paradox." If states gave temporary workers equal rights, then employers would be less likely to hire them. The result is that refusing to treat temporary workers as equals actually increases their economic well-being (Chang 2003).

As mentioned earlier, temporary worker programs vary widely. The *kafala* system is particularly notorious for abusive treatment of workers. Domestic workers around the world are also particularly vulnerable. In the United States, the National Domestic Workers Alliance documents the exploitation, abuse, and social isolation of many domestic workers (National Domestic Workers Alliance 2012). Low pay, lack of benefits, and little control over working conditions frequently combine with verbal, psychological, physical, and sexual abuse. Domestic workers often do not enjoy the same legal rights as other workers or are unable to access them.

If our only concern were economic inequalities, well-designed, carefully monitored temporary worker programs could go some way to address them. The fundamental problem with these arguments that attempt to justify immigration restrictions due to considerations of distributive justice is that they conceive egalitarianism primarily in terms of distributing resources. They fail to address the deeper, categorical inequalities that immigration regimes impose. In particular, they ignore how temporary migration programs fail to treat immigrants as moral equals, worthy of equal respect. Joseph Carens has observed that the existence of temporary worker programs depends on a "deliberate element of unfairness" (Carens 2013: 124). In particular, they create a group of people who receive fewer rights and are excluded from opportunities so that they can be exploited. These categorical inequalities are often further achieved through racialization. It may be that migrants may prefer exploitation, given the available alternatives. Nonetheless, this is not compatible with a commitment to equality.

In *Civil Ideals*, Rogers M. Smith predicted:

> Liberalizing and democratizing civic reforms will not come steadily and almost automatically, but only when economic, political, and military factors create overwhelming pressures for change. Defenders of ascriptive inegalitarian arrangements will not lack for arguments recognized as intellectually

respectable and principled; they will not always lose political struggles; and when they lose they will have opportunities to design new systems of ascriptive inequality recapturing some desired features of older ones, such as overall white supremacy. (Smith 1997: 9)

Immigration policy is an instance in which defenders of ascriptive inegalitarian arrangements or—to use the terminology of this chapter—categorical inequalities are threatening to win the political struggle. We should respond by insisting that categorical inequalities are not compatible with moral equality; instead, we need open borders.

NOTES

1. These arguments assume that economic growth is by and large positive, a view that is challenged by some environmental ethicists and radical political philosophers who advocate for a fundamental reorganization of economic and social institutions. In contrast, my point of departure is mainstream, liberal political philosophy. I am sympathetic to more radical political philosophy and to "no borders" arguments that challenge capitalism and the state-based international system. In *Toward a Cosmopolitan Ethics of Mobility: The Migrant's Eye View of the World* (2018c), I argue for a more fundamental reconsideration of borders and social organization, in large part because of the injustices inflicted by states and corporations—including environmental degradation that forces people to move. I limit my task here to a more modest task of defending open borders for a world in which states and private property are dominant institutions. I believe many of the arguments in this book will support or at least be compatible with a more radical perspective.

I thank Michael Neu for pushing me to address this point.

2. *Chae Chan Ping v. United States*, 130 U.S. 581 (1889).

3. *Ekiu v. United States*, 142 U.S. 651 (1892).

4. *Fong Yue Ting v. United States*, 149 U.S. 698 (1893).

5. The phrase "low skill" is prevalent in the economic literature to refer to poorly remunerated work that doesn't require postsecondary education. In fact, much of this necessary labor requires unacknowledged, specialized skills.

6. Borjas (2015) has argued that a more fine-grained analysis does in fact show a substantial decrease in wages of low-skilled workers. Clemens and Hunt (2017) respond, arguing that there are fundamental flaws with Borjas's data.

7. Other political theorists who endorse versions of this view include Cavallero (2006), Kukathas (2003), Miller (2017), Rawls (1999: 9), and Shachar (2009).

8. For a similar statement, see the Tripoli Declaration on Migration and Development (i.e., Joint Africa-EU Declaration on Migration and Development [Tripoli, November 22–23, 2006]), available at http://www.unhcr.org/refworld/docid/47fdfb010.html and Böhning and Scholeter-Paredes (1994).

Chapter 4

The Inherent Violence
of Border Controls

Eighteen-year-old Francisco Erwin Galicia's ordeal began when Border Patrol agents detained him with his seventeen-year-old brother Marlon on their way to a soccer scouting camp. Though Texas-born Francisco showed officers his state ID, Social Security card, and birth certificate, they brought him to the South Texas Detention Facility in Pearsall, Texas. The overcrowded holding area housed sixty other men, many sick, who had to sleep on the floor with aluminum-foil blankets (Mills Rodrigo 2019).

When Francisco asserted his rights and asked to make a phone call, officers told him that, "You don't have rights to anything" and threatened to charge him for falsifying documents (Puckett 2019). After two days, Marlon—who did not have legal residence—signed a deportation paper. Francisco was held for twenty-three days during which he was not permitted to shower. When he was released he had lost twenty-six pounds. He said: "It was inhumane how they treated us. It got to the point where I was ready to sign a deportation paper just not to be suffering there anymore. I just needed to get out of there" (Del Valle 2019).

Francisco's tribulation is a microcosm of the ills of immigration enforcement from the lack of due process that allowed a US citizen to remain behind bars for twenty-three days and to the abuse of detained migrants, calculated to pressure them to agree to deportation. It also illustrates how the Border Patrol targets and profiles Latinos as part of a racialized system of oppression.

So far I have appealed to philosophical arguments based on principles of freedom and equality to justify open borders, connecting the role of state border controls in creating categorical inequalities embedded in systems of domination and oppression. This overlooks the specific, concrete ways in which immigration laws are enforced. People directly affected by raids and deportations often have little patience for philosophical arguments. Immigrant

51

communities do not register their plight primarily in terms of lost opportunities or restricted freedoms (though these are real) but as palpable fear that family members may not return at the end of the day. Immigrant communities and their advocates are more likely to focus on deportation, detention, and systemic racism, rather than on abstract arguments for open borders. Some believe that the call for open borders distracts from more concrete injustice or plays into the hands of anti-immigrant politicians and their supporters.

Philosophical arguments may indeed seem less salient than concrete measures protecting the rights and well-being of immigrants. Nonetheless, these concrete wrongs that immigrants and their communities suffer daily are connected to open borders. A just migration regime without open borders is a mirage: immigration policy is founded on morally problematic differences between people. Its connection to racialization and racism encourages dehumanization and violence against migrants. Moreover, the means needed to prevent people from moving are disproportionate to any wrongdoing committed by illicitly crossing a border or overstaying a visa.

This chapter takes a different tack from the previous two chapters by focusing on the concrete realities of immigration enforcement. Even if we reject arguments based on freedom or equality for open borders, we need to ask about the means by which immigration is regulated and the predictable consequences of immigration control. Fleeting attention to the nature of border controls reveals their considerable violence. Border controls predictably contribute to the deaths of thousands of migrants each year, deliver refugees into the hands of their persecutors, and deprive hundreds of thousands more of their liberty through immigrant detention. Given the nature of border controls and the unlikelihood of reforms that would ameliorate these harms, immigration restrictions cannot be justified.

THE INHERENT VIOLENCE OF BORDER CONTROLS

Reece Jones powerfully exposes the direct and structural violence of state borders (Jones 2016: 8). This violence is clearest when security forces injure, detain, torture, and kill migrants as in the tragic case of fifteen-year-old Sergio Hernandez Guereca, shot by Border Patrol Agent Jesus Mesa Jr. (Jones 2016: 29–31) or fifteen-year-old Felani Khatun, one of over a thousand Bangladeshi civilians killed by India's Border Security Force (Jones 2016: 56–61). It is also visible in the EU partnership with countries such as Libya and Sudan to prevent migrants from reaching EU territories. By doing so, the EU participates in human rights abuses. In Sudan, this includes torture and extortion (Chandler 2018; Kingsley 2018; Suliman 2017). In Libya, migrants routinely face arbitrary detention under horrific conditions, slavery, physical and sexual violence (United Nations Support Mission in Libya 2018).

Even when agents enforcing immigration controls do not directly inflict violence, it is embedded in the migration regimes. The International Organization for Migration's Missing Migrant Project reports 4,737 deaths in 2018, almost half in the Mediterranean.[1] This is down from 6,280 deaths in 2017 and 8,070 deaths in 2016. These numbers represent reported deaths; the actual number of deaths is significantly higher. The ongoing lethality of the Mediterranean has led Maurizio Albahari to identify the deaths of migrants as "crimes of peace" (Albahari 2015: 21). Crimes of peace are committed under conditions of structural injustice and asymmetrical power. They are a product of callousness, willful ignorance, negligence, and failure of imagination that have lethal consequences for their victims.

In North America, the construction of the border wall under President Clinton's "Operation Gatekeeper Project" gave rise to the "funnel effect," with immigrants being driven to increasingly dangerous routes. The "funnel effect" was accurately predicted before the construction of the wall. Migrants died in the desert before the wall was constructed and it was clear that forcing them to pay smugglers to take more arduous routes during blistering days and freezing nights would add to this toll (Cornelius 2001). Migrant deaths are the most visible and horrific manifestation of border controls, but the other forms of violence

> are a direct outcome of a political system that seeks to control access to resources and limit movement around the world. Taken together, borders should be seen as inherently violent, engendering systematic violence to people and the environment. (Jones 2016: 10; see also Slack et al. 2016)

In both the Mediterranean and the United States, government officials have attempted to deflect the blame to smugglers or to the migrants themselves. This is a feeble attempt to absolve themselves not only of creating conditions in which violence is predictable but also of continuing to impose these conditions even after they begin to take their lethal toll. Jason de León writes:

> Contrary to the Border Patrol's sterile language ("Prevention Through Deterrence"), feigned naiveté ("this policy has had the *unintended* consequence of increasing the number of fatalities along the border"), and deflection of blame ("Not a day goes by when we don't find immigrants who say they were abandoned by their smuggler"), it is the federal agency that has created an infrastructural funnel along the US-Mexico border that intentionally directs people toward the desert. (de León 2015: 66)

States also inflict violence directly through immigration raids and immigrant detention. Bill Ong Hing examines the raid on the Swift meatpacking plant in Marshalltown, Iowa. ICE agents with warrants for a few individuals raided an entire plant, detaining all the workers for the day and dividing them into "documenteds" and "undocumenteds." Hing quotes attorney Sonia Konrad:

> ICE agents "conducted themselves as if they were dealing with terrorists entering the premises in uniform, black, jackets, strapped down guns, shouting and leaving no doubt to all workers that . . . they were not free to go." (Hing 2009: 9)

Local residents "labelled the ICE action as nothing short of 'Gestapo tactics' " (Hing 2009: 9). John Bowen, general counsel for the United Food and Commercial Workers, observed that " 'race was, almost without question, the sole criteria for the harsher interrogations' to which workers were subjected at the Greeley, Colorado plant" (Hing 2009: 13). Hing reports that "more than one individual was told, 'You have Mexican teeth. You need to go to that line [for undocumented persons] and get checked' " (Hing 2009: 1–2).

The effects of raids on individuals and communities are devastating. Raids invariably affect not only illegalized immigrants, but many US citizens and legal aliens who are interrogated and detained without access to legal counsel or the opportunity to notify family members. During the New Bedford, Massachusetts raid, around a hundred children were abandoned with other caregivers when their mothers were detained. Hing quotes Dr. Amaro Laria from the Harvard Medical School:

> "One of the most well established facts in mental health is that abrupt separation of children from their parents, particularly their mothers, are among the most severely traumatic experiences that a child can undergo." He testified that in the case of the raid, the "traumatic separations [were] perpetrated and sanctioned by our nation's law enforcement agencies, ironically in the name of protecting citizens." In his opinion, ICE had engaged in terrorism against these families and children." (Hing 2009: 16)

Then there are the broader effects on communities. Raids undermine trust in immigrant communities who refuse to report abuse or crime to the police.[2] It encourages racial profiling in which employers are reluctant to hire legal immigrants and citizens identified with immigrant groups. As José Jorge Mendoza emphasizes, "Not all citizens are affected by internal immigration enforcement in the same way" (Mendoza 2017: 106). He points to "[the] disconnection between what the majority experience in their own daily lives and how the collateral effects of internal immigration enforcement affect the lives of minorities, hides the true cost of enforcement" (Mendoza 2017: 109).

The violence of immigration raids goes beyond the actual raids. Even without actual militarized, Swift meatpacking-styled raids, the threat of raids inflicts psychological violence on immigrant communities. Only thirty-five people were arrested in the highly publicized ICE "Operation Border

Resolve" (Alvarez 2019). To label the operation a failure misses its intention: it was political theater, sending a message to nativists and to immigrant communities. It signals to nativists that borders are under control and that the government will continue to uphold white supremacy; it simultaneously tells immigrants—with and without legal status—that they do not belong and their lives are precarious, subject to state violence at any time.

Another violent tool of immigration enforcement is detention. The US incarceration of Central American children fleeing violence is the *reductio ad absurdum* of the securitization of borders (Lind 2019). More generally, the detention of hundreds of thousands of migrants and refugees around the world is a moral atrocity that arises directly from treating human mobility as a security issue (Nethery and Silverman 2015). Immigrant detention is administrative detention, meaning that immigrants enjoy few of the procedural safeguards guaranteed to people accused of crimes, including a right to an appointed counsel. Immigrants and refugees in detention frequently suffer physical assault, sexual abuse, and solitary confinement (Global Detention Project 2019). Australia and the EU outsource detention to other countries in full knowledge that migrants will suffer horrific human rights abuses (Farrell, Evershed, and Davidson 2016; United Nations Support Mission in Libya 2016). To incarcerate people for seeking better lives or attempting to escape persecution is disproportionately punitive and wasteful. It reveals either willful ignorance or a shattered moral compass. Worse, it is unavoidable that some people fleeing persecution will be detained and doubly traumatized, first by the regime that terrorized them, then again by the people from whom they sought help.

Public awareness of immigrant detention in the United States has increased, largely due to disturbing reports of the detention of children and of families. Nonetheless, detention continues to escape scrutiny, in part through the location of immigrant prisons (often in rural areas or in facilities that also house people incarcerated for nonimmigration offenses). Authorities also deflect attention through a variety of euphemisms such as "service processing centers," "family residential centers," and "tender age shelters" (Lima Marín and Jefferis 2019).

These euphemisms do not disguise the fact that immigrant detention is punitive (Chacón 2014). Detained immigrants are deprived of their liberty and separated from family members and communities. Already-traumatized asylum seekers are often further traumatized by confinement and by the deplorable conditions and treatment they receive. Many detention facilities lack adequate medical care and are rife with sexual assault, self-harm, and death (see, for example, American Civil Liberties Union, National Immigrant Justice Center, and Detention Watch Network 2016). The rise of immigrant detention coincides with the neoliberal transformation of the state, which includes an increasing reliance on private companies that profit from confinement (García Hernández 2017: 249). The companies not only receive public funds to detain and provide services to incarcerated immigrants, but they also in some cases profit from immigrant labor (Phillips 2017).

In practice, detention—including the fact that detainees often do not know when or if they will be released—is used as an incentive to convince immigrants to abandon legal claims to asylum or to appeal deportation. It is also used as a tool for deterring immigration.

HOW THIS CONNECTS TO OPEN BORDERS

The violence of immigration enforcement is undeniable, but why are open borders the appropriate response? Don't states have mechanisms short of open borders to reduce the harms to a morally acceptable level, allowing them to police their frontiers? Surely, partnerships with Libya and Sudan could be abandoned, detention could become an exceptional measure, and deportation could be carefully targeted with detainees provided with an adequate range of legal protections.

José Jorge Mendoza is sharply critical of the US immigration system but stops short of advocating open borders (2016). In his analysis, immigration enforcement operates in a state of exception, failing to meet widely acceptable standards of equal protection, due process under law, and judicial review. Governments have broad discretion to detain and deport immigrants without minimal procedures and protections guaranteed for citizens. Mendoza's solution is to move immigration policing out of a state of exception into the rule of law by granting immigrants the full protection of constitutional rights. He argues that what is needed to justify immigration enforcement is an "equality of burdens" standard under which selective enforcement would be forbidden. Mendoza's goal is for liberal democracies to live up to their own standards and to make immigration law consistent with commitments to freedom and equality.

If we followed Mendoza, the immigration system would need to be radically changed. Mendoza's approach would require scaling back immigration enforcement so that the burdens would be equally felt by white and nonwhite communities. Chandran Kukathas points out that "Joseph Carens famously opened his classic paper on open borders with the observation that borders have guards and guards have guns (Carens 1987: 251). What he did not fully recognize is that those guards are not just at the border and the guns mostly face inwards" (Kukathas 2017: 715). The reason why there is not more opposition to immigration enforcement is that enforcement targets minority groups. The majority white population would be unlikely to tolerate the routine violation of rights that minority groups endure because of immigration enforcement.

Mendoza's recommendations would also require transforming immigrant detention. At the very least, it would demand that the incarceration of immigrants be brought into line with incarceration for the nonimmigrant population. Immigrant detention lacks the procedural safeguards required to justify the deprivation of liberty. Immigration authorities have broad discretion on whether or not to detain people. In the United States, detained immigrants do not have a right to an attorney. Immigrant detention facilities are often located in rural areas, posing another barrier to legal and democratic oversight. Facilities frequently lack necessary services and amenities and are rife with abuse, in part due to the inadequate oversight. Immigrant detention reformers acknowledge these problems and propose concrete solutions (e.g., Human Rights First 2012; Migration and Refugee Services/United States Conference of Catholic Bishops, and Center for Migration Studies 2015). Their proposals include improving access to legal counsel, increasing court review and oversight, increasing the use of alternatives to detention, and replacing jails and prisons with facilities appropriate for civil immigration detention.

The problem with focusing on the concrete reforms is that they do little to mitigate the fundamental injustice of immigrant detention. Immigrant detention with access to a lawyer and the right to have one's detention promptly reviewed by a judge would still be wrong. The very practice of detaining immigrants rests on the conviction that it is acceptable to deprive some people of their liberty solely because they lack legal status. A deeper concern is that the focus on reform legitimizes the inexcusable, justifying oppression by giving it a human face. As García Hernández puts it, "Reforms, no matter how radical, that fail to grapple with this underlying moral perspective cannot successfully dismantle the violence at the heart of each of these institutions" (2017: 263).

Nonetheless, it should be possible to create a much more humane immigration system without open borders. Such a system would need to expand opportunities to migrate and reduce enforcement, largely eschewing disproportionate measures such as detention and deportation and openly tolerating unauthorized presence. Immigration violations, if not decriminalized altogether, would genuinely be treated as civil issues, more akin to parking tickets. Long-residing denizens without legal status would have a straightforward pathway to earn permanent residence and, eventually, to citizenship. These changes would be reason to celebrate. Why, then, take a further step toward open borders?

The first reason is that the much more humane system that I just described is only a small step away from open borders. An immigration policy genuinely compatible with liberal principles of freedom and equality supported by due process and nondiscrimination would be far more open. Why, then, not take the last step and endorse open borders instead, abolishing the opposition between people who belong to our community and potentially problematic "others?" A second reason is the difficulty of reaching this humane system while maintaining the right to exclude. Liberal criticism of immigration enforcement begins to identify important wrongs, but it ignores how immigration enforcement is a product of structural injustice. The liberal approach mischaracterizes the relationship between immigrants and dominant communities. Liberal theorists have analyzed the moral arbitrariness of place of birth and the troubling fact that it leads to vastly inequitable opportunities and to starkly different treatment. Unfortunately, the focus on moral arbitrariness leads them astray. Immigrant exclusion should not be analyzed as primarily a question about granting (or not granting) people outside of the community equal opportunities, suggesting that receiving states are passive bystanders reacting to strangers seeking entrance. Rather, it has always involved actively constructing people as inferior, subordinate, and exploitable to uphold racialized hierarchies.

Immigrant detention cannot be adequately understood without taking its context into account. It has evolved as part of a broader trend in which immigrants have been illegalized and criminalized. "Illegal" is a social and legal status, a result of policies which designate people as outside of or at the margins of the community, exclude them from full membership rights, and subject them to the threat of incarceration and deportation. Illegalization combines with criminalization, so that immigrants are increasingly under the purview of criminal law, including laws that make reentry after deportation a felony and that mandate deportation for a broad range of minor offenses (García Hernández 2013; Stumpf 2006). Immigration detention is also part of the larger trend of mass, racialized incarceration, so it must be brought into dialogue with broader abolitionist movements that emphasize how racialization and dehumanization are central to mass incarceration (Hernández 2011).

An adequate diagnosis of the wrongs of immigration enforcement needs to be informed by history. The racism of immigration policy is not a historical legacy that liberal democracies have overcome; rather, immigration policy continues to be motived by racism and closely bound up in structural racism that oppresses immigrants, as well as visible minorities identified with immigrant communities. Moreover, we need to pay attention to causality: what are the legal, social, and economic mechanisms that support the immigration system? What functional role do they play? As I argued in the previous chapter, it is not simply that opportunities are unevenly distributed, but the reason why they are unevenly distributed. This means turning our attention to structural injustice, which shows how race and class are not incidental to immigration enforcement; they are at the core of a system that allows for and indeed encourages the abuse, subordination, and exploitation of racialized, illegalized populations.

The logic of immigration enforcement limits the possibility of fundamental reform. Immigration systems can be more or less humane, but they all function by stigmatizing nonmembers and limiting their opportunities for the benefit of full members. For this reason, they are always vulnerable to xenophobes and political opportunists wishing to seize on the "us" versus "them" distinction at the core of their logic. Dehumanization and demonization are not aberrations but rather an ever-present potential response. The conviction that immigration can be justly regulated, at least in the long run, is naive. We may be able to do away with some of the more egregious injustices of the immigration system, but we need to abolish the system itself to achieve justice.

NOTES

1. See Missing Migrants Project, http://missingmigrants.iom.int/.

2. Abigail Andrews provides a disturbing enumeration of policies in North County San Diego, which included legal sanctions for hiring day laborers, banning residents from renting to illegalized immigrants, prohibiting parking in Latino neighborhoods, and checking migrants' status when responding to domestic violence calls (2018: 77–90).

Chapter 5

Arguments for Closing Borders 1: Self-Determination, Security, and the Environment

So far I have made the case that commitments to freedom and equality support open borders. Though I have addressed some objections in the process of doing so, readers may respond that I have neglected the most formidable objections to open borders. Not all opposition to open borders can be put down to prejudice or a failure to consider arguments for openness. A case for open borders must show that competing considerations do not override the right to freedom of movement or permit contemporary border regimes to impose arbitrary inequalities.

An immediate reaction many people have to the possibility of open borders is that they would have disastrous effects for wealthy countries. Surely, open borders would lead to hundreds of millions of people moving to richer countries overnight with devastating results for the economy, social institutions, and the environment. Democratic senator Bernie Sanders succinctly states this concern:

> If you open the borders, my God, there's a lot of poverty in this world, and you're going to have people from all over the world. And I don't think that's something that we can do at this point. Can't do it. So that is not my position. (Morin 2019)

Across the Atlantic, Rupert Read, then Green Party transport spokesperson, voiced a related set of concerns: "High levels of immigration create a more divided society, socially and economically, and ecologically weaker and less resilient" (Read 2014).[1] People worry about how open borders would affect their communities, cultures, and way of life. Significant levels of immigration will change communities. Even people who believe that migration enriches cultures and creates opportunities may be concerned about the rate of change. A large number of immigrants entering over a short period might undermine strong communities, reduce solidarity and social trust, and strain economic and ecological resources. These concerns lead to support for at least partial closure of borders, allowing states to restrict and to regulate immigration.

The second objection to open borders focuses less on their alleged effects, instead stressing values such as communities' right to self-determination. Communities have broad rights to set policies according to their interests and values. Part of self-determination involves determining membership through immigration policies. In the strongest versions of the self-determination argument, states have unilateral rights to exclude most immigrants if they choose.

In this chapter, I first analyze arguments for immigration restrictions based on self-determination. State rights to self-determination depend on the legitimate purposes that the state is pursuing, the impact of immigration on achieving these purposes, and the rights and interests of immigrants themselves. Second, I turn to two prominent objections: (1) open borders are incompatible with security and public order and (2) border controls are necessary to regulate population growth and to protect the natural environment. Chapter 6 addresses claims that immigration controls are legitimate because sedentary populations have legitimate interests in shaping their public culture, because of the need to maintain social trust needed to support the welfare state and because they are infeasible and thus incompatible with a realistic immigration policy.

STATE SELF-DETERMINATION

The most direct way to resist open borders is to appeal to communities' rights to self-determination. Communities (or their representatives) have the right to make decisions about their laws, policies, and projects. Though decisions should be constrained by considerations of justice and morality, communities ought to enjoy broad discretion in governing themselves. Among the most fundamental decisions for any community is how to determine membership (Walzer 1983). One strategy for resisting open borders is to argue that community rights and interests in deciding membership override the competing rights and interests of immigrants seeking admission.

Different grounds can be provided for self-determination and its implications for immigration. Perhaps states can invoke collective property rights to justify restricting immigration. After all, individual property owners have extensive, unilateral rights to exclude people from their property, even when this interferes with freedom of movement and opportunity. Perhaps the analogy from individual property rights can extend collectively, grounding state rights to restrict immigration. Ryan Pevnick proposes a sophisticated variation of the self-determination argument based on property rights (Pevnick

2011). In his "associative ownership view," community members acquire collective ownership rights through their contribution to the maintenance of state institutions. These rights in turn give communities a presumptive right to exclude immigrants, subject to considerations of global justice (e.g., severely impoverished immigrants' subsistence rights override the presumptive right to exclude).

One challenge with this account is that collective property rights are complex and their connection to immigration control is difficult to determine (Sager 2012b). It is unclear how collective property rights are acquired and what collective owners are entitled to. In some understandings, collective property rights may actually ground a right for people to immigrate. For example, Michael Blake and Matthias Risse have articulated an account of collective ownership of the earth's resources that would give many people, as co-owners of the earth's resources, a right to immigrate (Blake and Risse 2009). Furthermore, if the purpose of exclusion is to protect the collective goods that people produce, immigrants can retort that they do not interfere with people benefiting from collective property. Since the effect of immigration on public goods is often negligible and immigrants will soon begin contributing to state institutions, it would make more sense to delay their right to some public benefits rather than exclude them from the territory.

Even if collective property rights support excluding would-be immigrants, who should be making the decision to exclude? Pevnick wants to exclude illegalized immigrants and people outside of the state from collective ownership. This is hard to justify as illegalized immigrants and some people outside of the state pay taxes and contribute in other ways to the community. In Pevnick's own account, it would seem that the very people he hopes to exclude have claim to collective ownership. This has led Shelley Wilcox to identify a troubling circularity: self-determination rights are justified by collective ownership; but collective ownership rights are in turn determined by community's rights to self-determination (Wilcox 2012).

Another prominent argument comes from Christopher Heath Wellman, who derives a strong right to exclude immigrants from freedom of association (Wellman 2008; Wellman and Cole 2011). In his analysis, legitimate states have a right to self-determination. A core aspect of self-determination is freedom of association, which Wellman contends entails a right to dissociation—people should not be compelled to associate with others against their will. The freedom to dissociate built into self-determination permits states to unilaterally determine their immigration policies, overriding migrants' rights to freedom of movement or egalitarian obligations to ameliorate inequalities between states.

Wellman builds his argument using analogies to intimate relationships and to clubs. People have the right to unilaterally choose not to marry. Wellman extends this analogy to larger types of associations. Clubs; businesses; and religious, political, and professional groups often exercise broad discretion in excluding people. Wellman believes that the freedom to dissociate extends to states, which have a broad right to exclude immigrants.

A number of concerns about Wellman's account arise immediately. In particular, why does the national community get to exercise *its* freedom of association over other communities? Many groups have rights to freedom of association (Steiner 2001). Transnational families may wish to reunite in one location. Businesses may want to bring in workers from around the world. Nongovernmental organizations may want to sponsor refugees. Religious and ethnic groups have interests in bringing together members of their community. More broadly, attitudes toward immigration at the neighborhood or city level may be quite different from the policies of the nation-state. On what grounds should we privilege the state's freedom of association, especially over intimate relationships in families and other small groups? When we take seriously the number of associations that have strong interests in uniting and recruiting members, freedom of association might in fact justify far more immigration than states permit.

Wellman may also overstate the extent that freedom of association in fact entails a right to disassociation. People have a right to choose their spouse (and, correspondingly, not to enter into intimate relationships). They do not have a right to choose their sister-in-law or brother-in-law. A similar point holds for businesses, churches, and professional societies: individual members or subgroups in all of these associations often have broad rights to welcome new members. Those who would prefer not to associate with these new members do not have a right to exclude them; rather, if they prefer not to associate with them, their main recourse is to exit the group.

More generally, even if the case for a right to exclude in intimate relationships and for small organizations is plausible, it is not clear that this analogy extends to states. To determine this, we need to analyze freedom of association and its implications for exclusion in more detail. Stuart White argues that rules of exclusion can be justified if they protect people in pursuing the primary purposes of their association (White 1997). A trade union has a right to exclude management from its membership because this is necessary to protect its collective bargaining rights.

This right to exclude is only a presumptive right. We also need to ask if rules of exclusion deprive others of access to basic opportunity interests, under which White includes economic opportunities, community participation, and not being stigmatized by exclusion. In particular, categorical exclusion can violate the dignity of individuals by stigmatizing those who are excluded, particularly in societies in which some groups are assigned status inequalities (e.g., through sexism, racism, or homophobia). Trade unions should not have a right to exclude women, people of color, or LGBTQ people, even if the majority of their members are sexist, racist, or homophobic.

White offers a final qualification: even exclusions that affect basic opportunity interests can be justified in associations that protect the freedom of intimate association or protect freedom of conscience, expression, religious belief, and other considerations fundamental to one's moral personality. Bigots are free to not marry people from groups they despise. Christians can exclude atheists from their congregations. It should be stressed that though these groups have a right to exclude these groups, this does not necessarily entail that they are ethically justified in excluding people. Bigots who exercise their rights to not form associations based on their prejudices behave in a morally noxious manner.

To summarize, there is a right to freedom of association to protect the primary purposes of an association. This right is tempered by others' interest in accessing basic opportunities. In turn, an interest in accessing basic opportunities may be overridden if the association protects people's moral personality. The upshot is that freedom of association and any corresponding right to dissociate are complex and dependent on the nature of the association. To determine whether states have a right to exclude immigrants, we need to inquire further into the nature and purposes of the state.

Too often, arguments to restrict immigration characterize the state as a community with a unified, common will. Analogies to families and clubs (Walzer 1983; Wellman 2008; Wellman and Cole 2011) encourage this misrepresentation, obscuring the extent to which states are complex bureaucracies negotiating competing interests against a background of material and social inequality and power differentials (Kukathas 2012). Immigration policy is shaped in response to the demands of pro- and anti-immigrant lobbyists, businesses, community organizations, and individual constituents (Haas, Natter, and Vezzoli 2018). Far from accurately tracking the preferences of the majority, immigration policy frequently diverges from public opinion, instead responding to interest groups who place high salience on immigration issues (Freeman 2006; Hampshire 2013).

Furthermore, insofar as nation-states are communities at all, they are imagined communities (Anderson 2016). Even in small states, most people will never directly interact. Association with new members is mostly mediated through impersonal institutions. In most states, people can largely avoid directly associating with new members (indeed, the fact that many people have limited contact with immigrants is a damaging cause of prejudice [Pettigrew and Tropp 2006]). The right to dissociate is most compelling in intimate relationships and may not even apply at the state level.

What White's analysis indicates is that determining whether or not there is a plausible state right based on self-determination to restrict immigration requires a clearer account of the nature of the state and its purposes. One of the most fundamental purposes of the state is to guarantee the security of its members and to ensure public order. Members of states also have an interest in protecting the environment and may have an interest in regulating population levels. If open borders threatened security, public order, or the environment, there would be strong grounds for regulating it.

SECURITY AND PUBLIC ORDER

In April 2018, BBC 4 aired Enoch Powell's full "Rivers of Blood Speech" as part of a program *50 Year On: Rivers of Blood*.[2] In this notorious 1958 speech, Powell quotes a constituent, a "middle-aged, quite ordinary working man" who predicted that "in 15 or 20 years' time the black man will have the whip hand over the white man." Powell went on to proclaim:

> It almost passes belief that at this moment twenty or thirty additional immigrant children are arriving from overseas in Wolverhampton alone every week—and that means fifteen or twenty additional families of a decade or two hence. Those whom the gods wish to destroy, they first make mad. We must be mad, literally mad, as a nation to be permitting the annual inflow of some 50,000 dependents, who are for the most part the material of the future growth of the immigrant-descended population. It is like watching a nation busily engaged in heaping up its own funeral pyre.
>
>   . . .
>
> Here is the means of showing that the immigrant communities can organize to consolidate their members, to agitate and campaign against their fellow citizens, and to overawe and dominate the rest with the legal weapons which the ignorant and the ill-informed have provided. As I look ahead, I am filled with foreboding. Like the Roman, I seem to see "the River Tiber foaming with much blood."[3]

The BBC insisted that the choice to broadcast the speech was part of "a rigorous journalistic analysis of a historical political speech" and "not an endorsement of [Powell's] controversial views" (BBC 2018). Nonetheless, Labour peer Andrew Adonis asked the BBC to cancel the broadcast on the grounds that "Powell's speech is an incitement to racial hatred and violence which should not be broadcast" (Sweney 2018).[4]

Powell's speech has become a touchstone for immigration restrictionists. Former US presidential candidate Pat Buchanan wrote, "History suggests Powell spoke truth to power" (Buchanan 2006: 189), citing as evidence the May 2001 riots in England. Buchanan also invoked Jean Raspail's dystopia *The Camp of the Saints* (1975) in which the wretched of the earth descend upon Europe and "emerge in an orgy of looting, rape, and pillage to overrun the fat rich lands of the West" (Buchanan 2006: 191). Buchanan links the 2005 *banlieu* riots in Paris to Raspail's novel. Back in the United States a decade later, Ann Coulter continues the tradition with her diatribe *Adios, America: The Left's Plan to Turn Our Country into a Third World Hellhole* (2016).

If dystopian scenarios were limited to Conservative and far-right circles, we might give them short shrift. But as we can see from the Bernie Sanders quote in the introduction, the fear that open borders will be disastrous is shared across the political spectrum. Liberal egalitarian Brian Barry predicted that under open borders, mass immigration would lead to the collapse not only of the welfare state, including the medical and educational services, but also of liberal democracy itself, "especially since uncontrolled immigration would create any number of situations of potential ethnic conflict" (Barry 1992: 282).

We need to make these claims more precise to evaluate them. Among the state's most fundamental functions are guaranteeing the security of its members and preserving public order. These authors can be interpreted as claiming that security and public order cannot be maintained with high levels of immigration, especially from poorer to richer countries. Their case seems to be built on two types of claims. First, immigrants themselves are a security threat or will act in ways that undermine public order. In this view, many immigrants are "criminal aliens" or potential terrorists. Second, while immigrants themselves are not necessarily threats, their presence will lead to potentially violent conflict with locals. Both of these claims connect immigration control with a third claim: security and public order are best achieved through restrictive immigration policies.

The problem with the claim that immigrants are prone to crime and terrorism is that it is not supported by the evidence (Wickes and Sydes 2018). Study after study refutes the myth of the "criminal alien" (Ewing, Martínez, and Rumbaut 2015). Legal and illegal immigrants had lower incarceration rates than native-born Americans in 2017 (a result also found in 2014 and 2016) (Landgrave and Nowrasteh 2019). A 2017 study that analyzed data in 200 US Metropolitan Statistical Areas from 1970 to 2010 found that immigration has a negative effect on property crimes, robbery, and murder, as well as no effect on assault (Adelman et al. 2017). Light and Miller's analysis of data across the United States from 1990 to 2014 concludes that the growth of the undocumented population does not increase violent crime (Light and Miller 2018). Sanctuary counties, far from exposing residents to immigrant crime, have fewer crimes than nonsanctuary counties (Wong 2017). Deportations do not appear to reduce violent offenses or property offenses (Hines and Peri 2019). Research in Belgium (Lafleur and Marfouk 2017) and Germany (Maghularia and Uebelmesser 2019) supports similar conclusions.

If anything, the illegalization of immigrants may contribute to crime by reducing trust in law enforcement (Wong et al. 2019). Joseph Carens calls for a firewall between law enforcement and immigration enforcement since immigrants who fear deportation are less likely to report crime and trust law enforcement (Carens 2013). For example, the Trump administration recently froze processing of T and U visas that allow immigrant victims of crimes such as domestic abuse, sexual assault, and trafficking to assist law enforcement (Penn 2019). It is hard to reconcile promoting immigration enforcement at the expense of prosecuting serious crime with a commitment to security.

All of this leads Anna Flagg to conclude that "the link between immigration and crime exists in the imaginations of Americans, and nowhere else" (Flagg 2018). Indeed, the more salient question is not "do immigrants cause a rise in crime" but, rather, "why do so many people believe that immigrants cause a rise in crime?" The belief that immigration is a threat appears to be more closely related to the perceived size of the undocumented immigrant population, rather than the actual size (Wang 2012). It also stems from media coverage that perpetuates a threat narrative about migration and communicates that crimes by immigrants are committed because they are immigrants (Berry, Garcia, and Moore 2015).[5] This is tied to the long-standing, ongoing racialized construction of immigrants as threats (Chávez 2013).

Another objection is that large numbers of immigrants entering during a short period of time might challenge public order independently of the characteristics of any individual immigrant. A common trope in political debates about immigration is that relaxing border control would lead to Western countries being "flooded" or "swamped" by immigrants (sometimes described as "swarms") (Hogan and Haltinner 2015). According to this trope, only restrictive border controls protect democratic institutions from collapsing and from liberal cultures becoming irrevocably transformed. These fears are at least partly rooted in Eurocentrism in which the West is seen as offering unmatched opportunities and quality of life sustained through its unique values or culture. Parochial reporting on immigration to Western nations that ignores South-South migration creates the illusion that only stringent border controls restrain tens or even hundreds of millions of people from "flooding" or "invading" the West. This alarmist prediction is dubious. It is unlikely that there would in fact be as many migrants as feared. Moreover, it presupposes that border controls are an effective way of preventing arrivals and settlement.

One Eurocentric myth is that people around the world want to live in the Western world. A 2012 Gallop Poll suggests that 640 million adults or 13 percent of the world population would migrate if they had the opportunity (Clifton 2012). About 150 million people expressed interest in migrating to the United States. We should be cautious about how to interpret these surveys. Expressing a desire to migrate is not the same as taking steps to do so. Migration requires resources, including money and knowledge. Most people are reluctant to uproot themselves from their community, language, and culture. Also, much migration is temporary or circular and many people who intend to settle abroad eventually return. Data on migration in the EU suggest that estimates of migration levels between countries may be overstated (European Commission 2014). According to a 2017 Pew Research Center poll, only 4 percent of the EU's population lived in a country in which they were not born (Pew Research Center 2017). Describing the "myth of invasion," migration scholar Hein de Haas writes:

> Millions of sub-Saharan Africans are commonly believed to be waiting in North Africa to cross to Europe, which fuels the fear of an invasion.
> The conventional wisdom underlying such argumentations is that war and poverty are the root causes of mass migration across and from Africa. Popular images of extreme poverty, starvation, tribal warfare and environmental degradation amalgamate into a stereotypical image of "African misery" as the assumed causes of a swelling tide of northbound African migrants. (Haas 2008: 1305)

In contrast to this myth, De Haas's research shows that the view that most migrants wish to come to Europe is false (e.g., many sub-Saharans have the Maghreb as their destination). More migrants move to neighboring African countries than attempt to enter Europe, North America, or Australasia. This should give proponents of the "mass migration myth" pause. Migrants around the world are most likely to move to adjacent countries and tend to continue their journeys only when there are no opportunities or if they are driven out. Similarly, people are more likely to migrate internally or to adjacent countries in response to violence or persecution.

Moreover, many scholars have identified structural demand for low-wage labor as a major cause of migration—migrants play a crucial economic role supported by powerful interest groups (Haas 2008). Migration is embedded in the global economy with many industries depending on foreign labor (Sassen 2008). People respond to incentives such as available work; not surprisingly, migrants move elsewhere if these incentives disappear. Another way of describing this is that many migrants are responding to "pulls" that determine their destinations, not simply to "pushes." The decline in the US population of illegalized migrants in 2008 and 2009 due to the recession supports this (Passel and Cohn 2016).

All of this suggests that the connection between restrictive border controls and migration levels is not straightforward. Rather than stopping migration, restrictive policies often divert it, leading migrants to find new and often more dangerous routes, driving up the costs of migration and lining the pockets of smugglers and corporations profiting from border control (Andersson

2014; 2016; Sanchez 2015). Border controls can also have the perverse effect of increasing settlement. For example, in the United States, the increase in the large numbers of unauthorized migrants was largely due to more restrictive border controls (Massey, Durand, and Pren 2016). People who would have migrated on a seasonal or short-term basis stayed because the cost of entry increased.

Finally, though we do not know the effects of significantly more people immigrating, immigrants compose 88 percent, 77 percent, and 74 percent, respectively, of the populations of the United Arab Emirates, Qatar, and Kuwait (Kirk 2016). There are many problems with the treatment of migrants in the Middle East. Nonetheless, the Gulf States have not collapsed into civil wars of all against all because of immigration. The security impact of migration is greatest on weak or failed states that are unequipped to adapt to migration or for that matter to regulate it (Adamson 2006). Strong, stable states are capable of adjusting to increased migration flows as we have seen in Germany, where the economic integration of over a million asylum seekers has been largely successful (Degler and Liebig 2017).

Similarly, there is nothing inevitable about ethnic conflict. Supposed ethnic conflicts are often not primarily a response to ethnicity *per se* but rather to competition over resources (Dancygier 2010). The conviction that conflict is bound to arise between people of different ethnicities also overlooks what Rogers Brubaker calls "groupism," "the tendency to take discrete, sharply differentiated, internally homogeneous and externally bounded groups as basic constituents of social life, chief protagonists of social conflicts, and fundamental units of social analysis" (Brubaker 2002: 164). Groupism disguises how the boundaries of ethnic groups are actively constructed and how ethnic categories are mobilized by political entrepreneurs for their ends. Nuanced analysis of violent ethnic conflict frequently reveals that the cause is not group ethnic or cultural differences but rather the actions of organizations that claim to act in behalf of the group. Ethnicity can be mobilized in conflicts but whether this happens is usually a matter of political choice, not an inexorable result of migration.

In sum, the treatment of immigration as a security issue is not grounded in the evidence. Worse, it is counterproductive and harmful. Far more serious than the possible threat immigration may pose is the very real threat of the securitization of migration control, the militarization of borders, and the militarization of minds. Border controls create networks that smuggle and traffic people. No one would turn to people smugglers if they could freely cross borders, so policing the border encourages criminality. It places migrants in the debt of criminal groups, exposing them to extortion, forced labor, and prostitution. It also gives state actors the power to rob and extort migrants with impunity.

Fears that mass migration will overwhelm Western states is largely based on Eurocentric misconceptions about the intentions of immigrants (e.g., most people want to live in a Western state) and about the effects of migration (e.g., it will lead to institutional collapse). This contributes to treating immigration as a security issue in which states need to be protected from the dangers of immigration rather than as an economic and social issue in which human mobility needs to be coordinated to promote its benefits and minimize its burdens.

THE ENVIRONMENT AND POPULATION CONTROL

In addition to stressing security or public order, immigration restrictionists frequently justify their position by invoking the need to protect the environment (Beck 1996). The anti-immigration group NumbersUSA builds its case for restricting immigration on the need to curb population growth and lists "Environmental Impact" and "Sprawl, Congestion, and Farmland" as "Immigration Problems."[6] Similar themes are found in the work of philosophers such as Philip Cafaro (2015) and David Miller (2005; 2016). Cafaro gives an extended argument to end "mass immigration" to the United States to "defuse America's population bomb" (2015: 157–76) in part by implementing "a moratorium on all non-emergency immigration (with exceptions made for legitimate political refugees and asylum seekers), or at least a moratorium on all non-emergency immigration by immigrants of working age" (2015: 179–80; see also Cafaro and Staples 2009).

According to Brian Barry, open borders would devastate the planet, with countries losing any incentive to check population growth or environmental threats. Wealthy countries overwhelmed by the mass movement of people will have been reduced to a "desperation-driven short-run view understandably characteristic of Third World governments." This means that these wealthy states will lose their capacity as *de facto* (though admittedly "not very honest") "trustees for the planet" (Barry 1992: 283).

Many of these arguments have their roots in Paul Ehrlich's *The Population Bomb* (1971) and Garrett Hardin's 1974 essay, "Lifeboat Ethics: The Case against Helping the Poor." Ehrlich and Hardin tapped into popular Malthusian prejudices, positing a simplistic relationship between population growth, famine, and environmental disaster. Hardin claims that providing food aid to starving people accelerates the destruction of the environment; similarly, open borders would lead hungry people to immigrate to rich countries, destroying the environment there (Hardin 1974). Paul and Anne Ehrlich claim, "The flow of immigrants into the United States should be damped, simply because the world can't afford more Americans" (Ehrlich and Ehrlich

1991: 62; cited in Angus and Butler 2011: 114; see also Miller 2016: 66), and David Miller speculates that open borders would permit governments to export excess population rather than undertake responsible measures encouraging birth control. Closed borders, then, serve as an incentive for states to limit national populations (2005).

These arguments depend on empirical claims about the effects of border controls on the environment and on fertility rates. We cannot just assume the causal relationship between immigration and the environment; rather, it needs to be supported by evidence. Immigration is thought to harm the environment because it leads to population growth. The relationship between population growth and the environment is complex, as is the relationship between immigration and population growth.

Population's causal relationship to environmental degradation or to carbon dioxide emissions is shaped by many factors. Advocates of immigration restrictions for environmental reasons seldom carefully attempt to articulate these causal relations. The fear that immigrants will adopt the high consumption lifestyle of the rich world is often used to justify preventing people who consume less from migrating. Though the claim that more immigration to the United States would increase emissions seems straightforward, this hasn't been confirmed by research.

Even if the relationship between population and environmental degradation is established, it is not clear that restricting immigration would be an effective solution (Muradian 2006). We need to consider the major sources of emissions and other environmental problems, the available policy measures, and their probable impact. Moreover, we need to take a global perspective. In determining environmental impact, we have to evaluate the effects of migration in both receiving countries and sending countries, many of which may be indirect. National solutions cannot fix environmental problems that cross borders.

Consider Miller's suggestion of a link between national birth control policies and emigration. Miller's claim is counterfactual: *if there were a policy of open borders, states would export their excess population rather than take measures to curb population.* It is difficult to know how to evaluate this, particularly given that open borders would alter economic and political dynamics on a global level. Many factors influence fertility rate, including female literacy levels, the average age of marriage, religious and cultural beliefs, as well as government natalist policies (including providing access to birth control) (Roser 2017). If immigration contributes to economic growth and the empowerment of women, open borders might actually decrease world population levels.

This is not to suggest that immigration never has ecological consequences but the consequences are seldom for wealthy states or caused by human mobility. Deforestation and soil degradation are problems in some refugee camps. This should not be seen, though, as reason to close borders. Rather, it points to the problem of forced immobility. One of the best ways to avoid these adverse environmental impacts is to integrate refugees into the larger population (Jacobsen 1997).

Leaving aside the empirical issues, the insistence that much of the world's population should remain in poverty to protect the environment is morally obtuse. It amounts to privileged people using force to preserve their privilege by excluding others so that they can continue their unsustainable lifestyle. Ian Angus and Samuel Butler label this "populationism," arguing that these arguments "focus on symptoms, not causes" and "shift the blame for climate change, and the burden for stopping it, onto the poorest and most vulnerable people in the world" (Angus and Butler 2011: 4).

In fact, forced migration due to climate change and environmental degradation supports much more open borders. Climate change is implicated in large-scale migrations ranging from Central Americans fleeing drought by migrating to the United States (Blitzer 2019) to people displaced in the Syrian civil war (Kelley et al. 2015). Populations besieged by extreme weather are often trapped or displaced within their countries, in dire conditions (Black et al. 2013). While the possibility of migration should not excuse governments, corporations, and other actors from a duty to address climate change so that people are not forced to move, no good arises from restrictive policies that prevent their escape.

David Miller has a less alarmist argument that focuses instead on the right of communities to limit immigration to promote ecological goals and population control:

> Members of a territorial community have the right to decide whether to restrict their numbers, or to live in a more ecologically and humanly sound way, or to do neither and bear the costs of a high-consumption, high-mobility lifestyle in a crowded territory. If restricting numbers is part of the solution, then controlling immigration is a natural corollary. (Miller 2005: 202)

Miller refers to considerations of housing, congestion, and the importance of preserving wildlife habitats (2005: 202) as legitimate considerations for restricting immigration. Again, we need to ask about the relationship between immigration and these goods. Need restricting immigration be part of the solution? Are housing shortages primarily driven by population growth or by limited investment in affordable housing, financialization and speculation, as well as stark inequalities in income and wealth? Is congestion best addressed by trying to lower the number of people living in the area or should governments invest in high-quality public transportation? Is population growth in fact a threat to wildlife habitats? Miller does not undertake the analysis necessary to answer these questions.

Furthermore, his move from alarmist arguments about the devastating effects of population growth to questions of lifestyle means that we need to balance the desire for these goods with the restrictions on human freedom and the inequalities imposed by immigration policy. Miller's concerns about population and the environment are not about protecting basic needs but rather about political communities' right to use immigration control as a mechanism for realizing preferences. Perhaps there are grounds for states to use immigration controls to promote the preferences of their populations even if this reduces immigrants' freedom and diminishes their opportunities. The next chapter turns to arguments for restricting immigration based on culture and on immigration's alleged effects on social trust and the welfare state. It also examines claims that open borders should be rejected because they are infeasible.

NOTES

1. Thanks to Chris Bertram for bringing Read's view to my attention.
2. See BBC Radio. 2018. "50 Years On: Rivers of Blood," April 14, 2018. https://www.bbc.co.uk/programmes/b09z08w3.
3. The Roman is Virgil and Powell alludes to Sibyl's prophecy in the *Aeneid* predicting war and the River Tiber flowing with blood.
4. See https://twitter.com/Andrew_Adonis/status/984456933141831680/photo/1.
5. Thanks to Michael Neu for raising this point.
6. See NumbersUSA. n.d. "Environmental Impact." https://www.numbersusa.com/problems/environmental-impact.

Chapter 6

Arguments for Closing Borders 2: Culture and Social Trust

States pursue social, economic, and cultural goals to benefit the people within their borders or to fulfill democratic mandates. These include cultural goals such as creating a national identity through mass education, political and sporting rituals, language policy, and the promotion of the arts. They also include goals such as providing economic security through pensions, unemployment benefits, and health care. Many critics of open borders worry that unrestricted immigration would interfere with states' ability to pursue these goals. Though these objections to open borders differ from more drastic fears that they will threaten security, undermine public order, or destroy the physical environment, they are nonetheless influential and widespread. In what follows, I examine calls to regulate immigration to preserve and shape culture and claims that immigration undermines the welfare state by reducing social trust. I end by reflecting on the claim that open borders are infeasible.

CULTURE AND VALUES

The British prime minister Boris Johnson invited widespread criticism with these remarks:

> I want everybody who comes here and makes their lives here to be, and to feel, British—that's the most important thing—and to learn English. And too often there are parts of our country, parts of London and other cities as well, where English is not spoken by some people as their first language and that needs to be changed. (Boris Johnson—quoted in Halliday and Brooks 2019)

Johnson equivocates between wanting everyone to learn English (something most immigrants do [Fernández-Reino 2019]) and lamenting that people do not speak English as their first language (demanding that people abandon their heritage and assimilate). In doing so, he promoted a vision of Britain incongruent with the complex identities of many of its citizens and residents. A reader of *The Guardian* responded that English (Anglo-Saxon) immigrants (whose ancestors began settling in Britain in the fifth century) would do well to learn Cymraeg, Gàidhlig, and Gaeilge, as well as respect the language of people who emigrated from territories of the British Empire and the British Commonwealth (Metcalfe 2019).

Despite the controversy, Johnson's view is shared by many people. Politics professor Eric Kaufmann claims that "we must accept that white majorities are a group like any other, whose conservative members have a non-racist cultural interest in slowing ethnic change and facilitating voluntary assimilation" (Kaufmann 2018). In the United States, Samuel Huntington gave voice to fears that Hispanic (mostly Mexican) immigration needed to be limited to prevent fundamental change to the (allegedly) Anglo-Protestant character of the United States (Huntington 2005). David Frum decries how that assimilation has become more difficult "when immigrants can remain easily connected to their place of origin—and when the native majority has lost confidence in a unitary American identity" (Frum 2019). He laments that "hyphenated Americanism . . . has become a tool of cultural power" and argues for both reducing immigration and selecting immigrants more carefully to promote assimilation (Frum 2019). In his view, this is needed "to restore to Americans the feeling of belonging to one united nation, responsible for the care and flourishing of all its people" (Frum 2019).

Culture continues to be used to determine immigration policies around the world through the indirect, imprecise proxy of nationality (Joppke 2005; Orgad and Ruthizer 2010). Opportunities to visit or settle are determined in many ways by citizenship. According to the Global Passport Power Rank, citizens of the United Arab Emirates can travel without a visa or receive a visa upon arrival to 174 countries in 2019; citizens of Afghanistan only have thirty countries accessible to them.[1] National origins affect not only the ability to travel but also the ability to acquire a work visa and to immigrate. Immigration is also determined by ethnic identity in policies such as Israel's law of return, as well as whenever rights to immigrate are based on family connections.

Philosophers have also used culture as grounds for exclusion with Michael Walzer defending regulating admission and exclusion because they are essential to "defend the liberty and welfare, the politics and culture of a group of people committed to one another and to their common life" (Walzer 1983: 39). According to Walzer:

> Admission and exclusion are at the core of communal independence. They suggest the deepest meaning of self-determination. Without them, there could be no

communities of character, historically stable, ongoing associations of men and women with some special commitment to one another and some special sense of their common life. (Walzer 1983: 62)

The need to defend the group's culture and to preserve "communities of character" suggests the legitimacy of considering culture in decisions about admitting or excluding people.

We should be wary about calls to select immigrants by culture, given immigration's racist history (Gerstle 2017; Hirota 2017; Okrent 2019). Nativists frequently conflate race-based and culture-based assertions about immigrants' character and the impossibility of their assimilation. This passage from Madison Grant's *The Passing of the Great Race* (1916) is not atypical:

These immigrants adopt the language of the native American, they wear his clothes, they steal his name, and they are beginning to take his women, but they seldom adopt his religion or understand his ideals and while he is being elbowed out of his own home the American looks calmly abroad and urges on others the suicidal ethics which are exterminating his own race. (Quoted in Serwer 2019)

Grant combines cultural traits by referring to ideals and religion with flagrant racism. Early twentieth-century jeremiahs against immigration in the United States would not be out of place in today's political life where culture continues to resonate in the arena of dog-whistle politics. Immigrants' alleged refusal to integrate, to learn the language, and to adopt majority values are frequently used to justify their exclusion.

Mainstream commentators are quick to repudiate any connection between concerns about culture and racism. Kaufmann refers to "non-racist cultural interests." In his book *Exodus*, Paul Collier insists:

Cultures are not genetically inherited; they are fluid clusters of norms and habits that have important material consequences. A refusal to countenance racially based differences in behaviour is a manifestation of human decency. A refusal to countenance culturally based differences in behaviour would be a manifestation of blinkered denial of the obvious. (Collier 2013: 21–22)

Collier attempts to reduce racism to the view that groups can be distinguished by their genetic inheritance and that this genetic inheritance determines their characteristics and behavior. This narrow definition of racism has never captured the ideology of racists, who freely blend supposedly biological features with ethnic and cultural traits as they denigrate and marginalize groups. Nor can we understand racism without investigating the construction of whiteness, which functions as an allegedly neutral standard against which "non-white" groups are measured (Mendoza 2016). The history of immigration, at least in the United States, is also a history of how some groups of immigrants such as the Italian and Irish came to be included as "white," whereas others such as the Japanese, Indians, or Hispanics became "non-white" (Jacobson 2002; Roediger 2006). Immigrant groups suffer discrimination and marginalization because they are conceived as nonwhite, not because of crude racist beliefs based on biology (though these are also present).

Indeed, Collier's conviction that culture and race can be untangled is belied by his remarks later in *Exodus* that "Nigerians radically, deeply, do not trust each other. Opportunism is the result of decades, probably centuries, in which trust would have been quixotic, and it is now ingrained in ordinary behaviour" (Collier 2013: 66). As a result of their culture, Nigerian immigrants "tend to be untrusting and opportunistic" (2013: 67). Collier's evidence for this sweeping generalization is his own experience of living in Nigeria and a study that found that diplomats from countries with high levels of corruption are more likely to commit parking violations when provided with immunity (Fisman and Miguel 2007). Collier's narrow understanding of racism allows him to unreflectively attribute fixed, across-the-board, negative qualities to a group of people without grappling with the moral implications. He goes on to justify limiting immigration, arguing that the sustainable rate of migration is determined by the distance between immigrant cultures and the culture of the indigenous population (Collier 2013: 262). Since family-based immigration can lead to the growth of the diaspora, migration policy should "[set] the rights to migration from particular countries so as to offset these perverse effects of cultural difference" (Collier 2013: 262). Collier and Kaufmann wrongly think they can tease apart discrimination based on culture and racism.

Furthermore, claims about cultural difference are conceptually fraught. Evaluating the legitimacy and justification of culturally based policies depends on what is meant. When Kaufmann and Frum insist that immigrants assimilate, we should ask *assimilate to what or to whom*? The term "culture" is vague and ambiguous. Social scientists use culture in mutually incompatible and possibly even conceptually incoherent ways (Smith 2016). Bhikhu Parekh observes, "When used *sans phrase* culture encompasses more or less the whole of human life" (Parekh 2002: 143). Narrower definitions of culture can be useful for particular purposes but need to be defended.

Furthermore, cultural selection is difficult to square with the fact that all societies are diverse—and in the case of Britain (as well as many other countries), possibly "super-diverse" (Vertovec 2007). When Collier compares the distance between immigrant groups' culture and the culture of the indigenous population, what is he comparing? Diversity is not something that only occurs between cultures, it is also internal to cultures, adding further complexity. Furthermore, cultures are continuously changing with immigration as only one of many drivers. Efforts to stop change are not only futile but likely self-defeating, as adapting to change is necessary for cultural survival (Scheffler 2007). Finally, if we take culture seriously as a criterion for shaping immigration policy, it may in fact turn out to support freedom of movement (Lenard 2010). Hundreds of millions of people around the world will have legitimate claims to belong based on cultural similarities.

Leaving aside the conceptual and practical problems, cultural selection is in many respects an illiberal project, discriminating against or imposing a particular way of life on people for morally illegitimate reasons (Wilcox 2004). It risks imposing a judgment that some cultures are inferior or undesirable, attacking people's dignity and self-respect. For this reason, philosophers such as Will Kymlicka, David Miller, Liav Orgad, and Michael Walzer attempt to circumvent these conceptual and moral issues by providing a more precise, defensible account of culture (Kymlicka 2001; Miller 2005; 2016; Orgad 2015). David Miller does this by distinguishing between private and public culture. Under private culture, he groups dress, food choices, personal relations, art, music, and religion (Miller 2016: 67). States can tolerate and even embrace diversity in private culture. Public culture, in contrast, refers to

> a shared (overlapping rather than identical) set of beliefs about the values the wider society should embody and pursue: how people should conduct themselves in public space, what the society should be proud of and what it should be ashamed of, what kind of political system it should have, what the future goals of society should be, and so on. (Miller 2016: 67)

Like Collier, Miller claims that "there needs to be a considerable degree of convergence [in public culture] if the society is going to function without serious conflict" (2016: 67). Though society can function despite considerable disagreements about private culture, he suggests that a stable state cannot be composed of an equal number of Democrats and theocrats (2016: 67).

While Miller is mostly focused on public culture, he worries that differences in private culture can affect shared public culture when "minorities retreat into enclaves with rather little contact with those from outside of their own community" (2016: 68). The members of these "parallel societies" (2016: 68) infrequently interact with people outside of their group, losing contact with the shared public culture. Miller believes this lowers intergroup trust and worries that in this case "it becomes harder to reach agreement on public matters because people approach them on the basis of conflicting and privately held beliefs and values—and with the possible alienating effect of separate and exclusive cultural identities" (2016: 68). Miller contends that avoiding the threat to public culture requires using immigration policy to determine the kind and scale of cultural diversity that new members potentially introduce (2016: 68).

Miller's account depends on a number of questionable claims, beginning with the assumption that ethnic enclaves reduce integration—access to a network and support system may actually foster economic integration (Martén, Hainmueller, and Hangartner 2019). Leaving that aside, how much agreement is there in actual democratic public cultures? In the United Kingdom and the United States, debates about race, colonialism, and empire suggest that people—*independently* of their ethnic or cultural identities—do not have an overlapping agreement on what their countries should be proud and ashamed of, let alone their society's future goals. That aside, do immigrant groups really diverge from the dominant group in their beliefs about public culture? Miller provides little evidence for this claim.

In fact, his remark that one cannot have a state made up of an equal number of Democrats and theocrats echoes ill-founded claims that European Muslims are theocrats hostile toward women's rights, gender equality, and LGBTQ communities, as well as to freedom of speech and democracy. This dynamic of "us versus them" is central to popular books such as Patrick Buchanan's *The Death of the West* (2002), Christopher Caldwell's *Reflections on the Revolution in Europe: Immigration, Islam and the West* (2010), Eric Kaufmann's *Whiteshift: Populism, Immigration and the Future of White Majorities* (2019), Douglas Murray's *The Strange Death of Europe: Immigration, Identity, Islam* (2017), and Slavoj Žižek's *Against the Double Blackmail: Refugees, Terror and Other Troubles with the Neighbours* (2016). Political philosophers are not immune from mimicking rhetoric that insists some values are particular or unique to Westerners. In her polemic "Is Multiculturalism Bad for Women?" Susan Moller Okin draws a sharp division between Western values (considered synonymous with liberalism or liberal democracy) and non-Western values which many immigrants purportedly endorse for cultural reasons (Okin 1999: 16–17).[2] Miller similarly remarks in a discussion about civic integration that "there are practices that immigrants may bring with them that liberal societies have a legitimate interest in outlawing: examples would include coerced marriages and the punishment of apostasy" (2016: 137).

In this view, large numbers of immigrants with patriarchal, anti-liberal, or antidemocratic values can undermine public culture because they do not subscribe to liberal or democratic norms or because they reject constitutional principles. The evidence presented for the claim that significant numbers of immigrants have these values is usually a series of anecdotes of people identified with a particular culture acting violently or oppressively; these anecdotes are meant to reveal widespread cultural beliefs and values. For example, dowry murders in India are often explained by culture, implying that they are endorsed by Indians as a group (an odd claim, given India's extraordinary diversity). As Lea Volpp points out, it makes more sense to see dowry murders as analogous to domestic violence murders in the United States rather than as a widely endorsed cultural norm (Volpp 2001: 1187).

Are there significant differences in the values people in different geographical regions endorse? Moreover, can value differences be meaningfully attributed to culture (as opposed to being primarily attributable to environmental factors)? This is not obvious. The suggestion that people in other parts of the world hold different values is usually a normative claim imposed by the person making this judgment rather than an impartial description of beliefs or practices. Defining and identifying values is a complex hermeneutic task that does not allow easy comparison between individuals and groups, especially across linguistic and geographical distances. Also, even if values do differ across geographical regions, this does not mean that the values of immigrant populations within Western states differ in significant ways from those of nonimmigrant populations. In both cases, survey evidence may initially appear to support differences but becomes less compelling upon further analysis.

Consider research on Muslim populations who are frequently portrayed as holding fundamentally different values. The connection between Islam and attitudes about democracy, war, and peace do not appear to have much explanatory power compared to economic and political factors (Tessler 2003). Though some research based on the World Values Survey suggests that Islamic populations have higher levels of support for patriarchal values (Alexander and Welzel 2011), it is difficult to establish if this support is caused by culture or by structural factors such as political or economic power relations. Some research concludes that Muslim identity contributes to an endorsement of patriarchal values, though it also reveals significant internal differences within Muslim societies (after all, there are many Muslim identities), as well as flexibility in values when the social environment changes. It also appears that education and employment reduce patriarchal values, especially among women, suggesting that adherence to values is not rigid and might be better explained by factors external to religious identity (Alexander and Welzel 2011).

In their analysis of the Gallup polls of the Muslim world, John Esposito and Dalia Mogahed find that Muslims and non-Muslims agree on most topics (Esposito and Mogahed 2007). The Pew Research Center's Division of US Politics and Policy reaches a similar conclusion. In fact, in 2011, Muslims Americans were also *more* likely to say that they want to adopt American customs and ways of life than the general public believes (56 percent versus 33 percent) with another 16 percent of Muslims claiming that they want to both adopt American customs and ways of life *and* be distinct from the larger American society (a claim consistent with many other immigrant groups who retain a cultural identity). US Muslims consider religion important in their lives (69 percent very and 22 percent somewhat) on par with US Christians (70 percent very and 23 percent somewhat) but (not surprisingly) less than the general public (58 percent very and 24 percent somewhat) (Pew Research Center 2011). About 81 percent of US Muslims believe that suicide bombing and other violence against civilians is never justified to defend Islam from its enemies (5 percent answered rarely, 7 percent answered sometimes, and 1 percent answered often) (Pew Research Center 2011). There was no parallel question about violence toward civilians for non-Muslim populations to allow for comparison (e.g., what do non-Muslims think about the deaths of civilians as "collateral damage" in US military campaigns?). On the whole, the beliefs and attitudes of Muslims are largely congruent with those of the majority, as well as with the significant part of the *general public* that disagrees with the majority. While Pew and Gallup research suggests some significant differences, these differences do not reveal a clear divide between Muslim and other populations.

The attribution of values to groups risks making an essentialist claim about the group, artificially homogenizing opinion, and ignoring how opinion has changed over the time—or may change in the future. This ignores how values are negotiated, contested, and reproduced, removing agency from members. It also risks attributing causality to culture without considering environmental factors.

More fundamentally, the idea of Western values rests on an indefensible division of the world. Culture and the values that supposedly accompany it are far more amorphous and dynamic than the pundits who mobilize them for political purposes usually allow. As Amartya Sen points out:

> There is a lot we can learn from studies of values in Asia and Europe, but they do not support or sustain the thesis of a grand dichotomy. Contemporary ideas of political and personal liberty and rights have taken their present form relatively recently, and it is hard to see them as "traditional" commitments of Western cultures. There are important antecedents of those commitments in the form of the advocacy of tolerance and individual freedom, but those antecedents can be found plentifully in Asian as well as Western cultures. (Sen 1999: 40)

History shows that culture has multiple origins spread across the globe for centuries (and across the Old World for millennia) through conquest, trade, and migration (Frankopan 2016; Hoerder 2011). Transnational and supranational connections are not merely historical artifacts. Many communities continue to persist across state borders (Levitt and Jaworsky 2007). Attempts to justify exclusion on the grounds of cultural distance perpetrate intellectually indefensible Eurocentric prejudices. We should abandon attempts to use immigration policy to share culture as incoherent and noxious.

SOCIAL TRUST AND THE WELFARE STATE

Perhaps exclusion is not justified by culture itself, but rather by the effect that large-scale immigration has on receiving societies. In this case, it may not be the characteristics of the immigrants but the perceptions and reactions of nonimmigrants or the effects of immigration independent of immigrants' culture. The economist Milton Friedman said, "It's just obvious that you can't have free immigration and a welfare state" (Brimelow 1997). Friedman himself favored free immigration and abolishing the welfare state, but many other people find this trade-off less appealing. David Miller has argued that one reason for restricting immigration is to preserve social justice within societies. Social welfare depends, in his view, on a high level of solidarity, something which he believes may not be possible in highly diverse societies. He follows Paul Collier (2013: 74–78) in holding that immigration reduces interpersonal trust (Miller 2016: 64). Collier, in turn, relies heavily on an influential paper by sociologist Robert Putnam on how diversity affects social capital (i.e., networks of social relations characterized by reciprocity and trust [Putnam 2001: 18–19]).

Putnam investigated two hypotheses about diversity: (1) the "contact hypothesis" that claims that diversity "fosters interethnic tolerance and social solidarity" (Putnam 2007: 141); (2) "conflict theory" that suggests that diversity, largely due to "contention over limited resources . . . fosters out-group distrust and in-group solidarity" (Putnam 2007: 142). He con- cluded, using evidence from the United States, that diversity does seem to cause out-group distrust. Surprisingly, it *also* appeared to produce in-group distrust, rather than in-group solidarity: "Diversity seems to trigger *not* in- group/out-group division, but anomie or social isolation" (Putnam 2007: 149). This leads him to conclude that "in the short to medium run . . . immi- gration and ethnic diversity challenge social solidarity and inhibit social capital" (Putnam 2007: 138).

Despite the influence of Putnam's article, his study has clear limitations, some of which Putnam himself identified. It only examines people at one point in time (American communities in the year 2000) and implies noth- ing about the effects of diversity and immigration over time (Putnam 2007: 158–59). Putnam does not connect his research to policies that reduce immi- gration. Indeed, he is careful to emphasize the benefits of immigration and that short-term trade-offs between diversity and community can be addressed by good policies (Putnam 2007: 164).

Subsequent research complicates, if not refutes, Putnam's conclusions. Research using cross-national data from twenty-eight European countries found no evidence that ethnic diversity leads to social isolation (Gesthuizen, van der Meer, and Scheepers 2009) and another study in Britain finds the relationship between diversity and trust weak and contingent (Sturgis et al. 2011). In the United States, Maria Abascal and Delia Baldassarri dispute Putnam's methodological assumptions and data analysis, finding in turn that "diversity is a negligible predictor of trust compared with classic sociological indicators of inequality" (2015: 754). Christel Kesler and Irene Bloemraad find that relationships between trust and engagement depend on the institutional and policy contexts and not on the level of diversity *per se* (Kesler and Bloemraad 2010; see also Pevnick 2009).

Even if we accept the empirical claim that sometimes immigration undermines social trust, leading in turn to less support for social benefits, it is not clear that restricting immigration is a morally permissible policy to protect the welfare state. First, as Ryan Pevnick points out, even if we think that a welfare state is important for a just society, the overall consequences of improving the lives of migrants might justify weakening it (Pevnick 2009: 6). Importantly, there is no evidence for Friedman's radical assertion that open borders would destroy the welfare state, only that high levels of immigration might reduce support. Second, arguments that predict bad outcomes because of how people will react are themselves suspect. They presuppose an unduly rigid view of human behavior, ignoring how people make decisions in institutional contexts that can be modified. The effect of immigration depends on the narratives that we tell about it, the policies we use to encourage positive contact between people, and the tactics we adopt to address challenges. Rather than limiting immigration, we should embrace diversity and design institutions that reap its benefits.

FEASIBILITY

A final objection to open borders is to deny their feasibility: even if open borders are an attractive ideal, they are not something that can realistically be achieved. Perhaps theorizing about open borders is a noble attempt to articulate a vision of a just world but ultimately provides little guidance for the here and now. More cynically, it is an idle fantasy indulged by philosophers who offer little for real-world politics.

Henry Sidgwick articulated this position in the nineteenth century, maintaining that under the cosmopolitan ideal, the state's role is to maintain order over its territory, "but not in any way to determine who is to inhabit this territory, or to restrict the enjoyment of its natural advantages to any particular portion of the human race" (Sidgwick 1897: 306). Though he affirms that this may be "the ideal of the future," he maintains that for now "it allows too little for the national and patriotic sentiments which have in any case to be reckoned with as an actually powerful political force, and which appear to be at present indispensable to social wellbeing" (Sidgwick 1987: 306; for discussion, see Zolberg 2012).

Sidgwick's convictions are echoed by today's critics of open borders (Miller 2016); they are also accepted by many open-borders advocates (Carens 1996, 2000, 2013; Kukathas 2005). Joseph Carens tells us that he does not intend his arguments to serve "as a concrete recommendation for current policies or ones in a foreseeable future" (Carens 2000: 643). Instead, his arguments are meant to serve "a heuristic function":

[The case for open borders] is important not primarily as a guide to what we ought to do in the here and now (because there is little we can do about these fundamental features of our world) but rather as a guide to how we ought to think about the fundamental legitimacy of the social arrangements that govern our lives. (Carens 2000: 643)

Thirteen years later, Carens continued to insist that "the idea of open borders is a nonstarter," citing the perceptions of many citizens of Europe and North America about immigration (Carens 2013: 229). According to Carens, citizens of rich states see open borders as potentially disastrous to their well-being. Moreover, the conviction that states have a broad moral entitlement to control immigration is assumed without question. As a result, no politician can advocate open borders and hope to remain in office (Carens 2013: 229).

The alleged infeasibility of open borders is rooted in misconceptions about their effects and lack of imagination about political possibilities. Open borders are a political goal that we should begin to work toward now. Though much of the world appears deeply inhospitable to migrants today (Vallet and David 2012), we should resist drawing conclusions based on a limited time horizon and selective attention to certain migration policies.

To evaluate the charge that open borders are infeasible, we will need to consider the many senses in which a theory can be feasible. If a political proposal is feasible, it must be possible to bring about what is proposed (Gilabert and Lawford Smith 2012). What does it mean for it to be possible to bring about something in a particular place and time? Pablo Gilabert and Holly Lawford-Smith (2012) analyze this question in terms of accessibility and stability. A feasible proposal must be accessible: in the case of open borders, there must be a series of steps that could be taken to achieve an open-border world. It must also be stable, enjoying sufficient support to endure for a reasonable period of time. As we have seen, many open-borders critics contend that if borders were opened, the result would be disastrous, either destabilizing the political regimes or triggering rapid efforts to slam the gates shut. If they are correct, open borders are not feasible.

Gilabert and Lawford-Smith distinguish various degrees and dimensions of feasibility. First, there are hard constraints. A feasible proposal must not violate the rules of logic or the laws of physics. We can safely rule out Charles Fourier's prediction that during the era of perfect harmony a boreal citric acid will flow into the sea and combine with salt, giving it the flavor of lemonade and contributing to the evolution of amphibious sea servants to pull ships and work in the fisheries (Fourier 1996; see also Cowen 2007: 1). More controversially, there may be constraints imposed by economics or human nature that rule out certain proposals. For example, David Hume insisted that a social system that neglected the role of scarcity and limited benevolence would not be a human possibility (Hume 2006). If he is correct, any proposal that violates these hard constraints is infeasible.

How might open borders violate hard constraints? Open borders do not violate the rules of logic or the laws of physics. Do they depend on unjustifiable assumptions about the world or about human psychology? For example, would open borders require levels of altruism among individuals and communities that go beyond what we reasonably think possible? Would natural limits on resources create scarcities so that they need to be distributed with strict control over membership? If the anti-immigrant Federation for American Immigration Reform is correct and countries really are analogous to lifeboats (Ruark and Martin 2009, cf. Hardin 1974), open borders would be for all practical purposes unachievable.

As we have seen, there is little evidence for hard psychological or economic constraints to open borders. Open borders do not require angelic benevolence and countries are not lifeboats. We know this because there are many historical and contemporary examples of open borders, including the EU, the Trans-Tasman Travel Arrangement between Australia and New Zealand, and the Nordic Passport Union (among Denmark, Finland, Iceland, Norway, and Sweden) (Casey 2010). The EU is the most well-known model, but we should also consider MERCOSUR Residence Agreement between Argentina, Bolivia, Brazil, Chile, Colombia, Ecuador, Paraguay, Peru, and Uruguay (Acosta Arcarazo and Geddes 2014). Nationals of the Southern Common Market (MERCOSUR) or Associate Member States who can provide identification and evidence of no criminal record for the previous five years are entitled to a two-year temporary residence permit that allows them to reside and work for two years. After two years, temporary residence permits can be transformed into permanent permits if the person can demonstrate resources to be self-sustaining (Acosta 2016). Another fascinating example is Ecuador's 2008 Constitution and its organic law on human mobility (*ley orgánica de la movilidad humana*), which sought to establish open borders (Government of Ecuador 2017). Though Ecuador faced many obstacles, including opposition from other states, and has since placed some

restrictions on human mobility, it retains some of the most open visa requirements in the world (Echeverri Zuluaga and Acevedo Sáenz 2018: 109–11;
Wheeler 2014).[3]

Critics who maintain that open borders are infeasible must therefore have
soft constraints in mind. The feasibility of most proposals is a matter of
degree; bringing them about is more or less difficult or likely. Soft constraints
include many economic, institutional, and cultural constraints, as well as constraints imposed by human psychology or motivation. These constraints are
malleable: motives shift and economic and political institutions and cultures
change.

One sense in which open borders might be inaccessible is that people in
power do not have the political will to move toward open borders. A common
explanation for lack of political will is that elected officials assume that their
constituents oppose open borders. Any mainstream politician advocating
open borders becomes unelectable. In turn, citizens in the developed world
may wish to preserve their privileges and believe that open borders would
expose them to unacceptable security risks or drastically lower their standard
of living. The likelihood of bringing about open borders could rise if we could
change people's beliefs about their effects. We should be particularly cautious to predict something is infeasible because of people's will, beliefs, or
attitudes—our very prediction reinforces the alleged inflexible mind-set that
prevents moving to a more just world.

Another objection is that immigration itself isn't the problem; rather, it is
the way that people predictably react to immigration. Natives have strong
convictions—or so the argument goes—that immigrants will "steal" their
jobs, absorb scarce social benefits, or transform their culture. Hilary Clinton articulates the concern that the public will reject generous immigration
policies:

> I admire the very generous and compassionate approaches that were taken par-
> ticularly by leaders like Angela Merkel, but I think it is fair to say Europe has
> done its part, and must send a very clear message—"we are not going to be able
> to continue to provide refuge and support"—because if we don't deal with the
> migration issue it will continue to roil the body politic. (Wintor 2018)

The perception that immigration is too high or out of control is fodder for far-
right or populist parties that use the "legitimate" concerns of natives to gain
support for their noxious policies. It is easy to be pessimistic about the modest immigration reforms, let alone open borders in today's political climate.
The election of leaders such as Donald Trump in the United States or Viktor
Mihály Orbán in Hungary and the rise of far-right, anti-immigrant parties
may seem grounds for despair. Nonetheless, we need to beware of confusing

extremist rhetoric with wide-scale public opinion and with neglecting how anti-immigrant language and policy may stem more from political parties seeking to gain power by attempting to shape the agenda by championing unpopular issues than from widespread public support (Grande, Schwarzbözl, and Fatke 2018).

An International Organization for Migration poll of over 183,000 adults in 140 countries between 2012 and 2014 found that globally 22 percent of people surveyed thought immigration to their country should be increased, 21 percent thought it should be kept at its present level, and 34 percent thought it should be decreased (with 22 percent responding Don't know Refused to Answer). In Oceania, 41 percent of those surveyed thought immigration should be increased; this figure was 34 percent in North America and 30 percent in Latin America (Esipova et al. 2015). This doesn't support open borders, but it does suggest more openness than often proclaimed. Attitudes supporting restriction may also be caused in part by false beliefs where the general public systemically overestimates the proportion of immigrants in their countries (Alesina, Miano, and Stantcheva 2018). Ironically, Vera Messing and Bence Ságvári find that European opposition to immigration is strongest in countries that have few immigrants. Rather than being a response to immigration, it is related to feelings of controlling one's own life and perceptions about whether the government is able to control migration (Messing and Ságvári 2019).

In fact, mainstream political parties frequently adjust their position on immigration as a reaction to the success of parties on the far-right, rather than as a response to broad public opinion (Abou-Chadi and Krause 2018). Furthermore, anti-immigrant attitudes may come explicitly from government policies that frame immigration as threat, rather from pre-existing public opposition (Mulvey 2010).[4] Though critics of open borders such as David Miller claim that voters' perception of recent refugee flows to Europe cause the unviability of more open immigration policies, people's attitudes toward immigration may be less influenced by current events than often thought (Kustov, Laaker, and Reller 2019).[5] The assumption that opening borders is infeasible is a self-fulfilling prophecy, rather than a sober judgment about political realities.

So far I have said little about the issue of stability. Stability will depend significantly on the effects of open borders. As we have seen in previous chapters, the question of open borders is often met with apocalyptic predictions. Little evidence supports these predictions, but even if we rule out environmental disaster or the collapse of political institutions, it would be hard to sustain open borders if they led to a significant decrease in the quality of people's lives. Stability requires widespread political support—or at least indifference.

Experiments with open borders provide valuable evidence that casts doubt on the most pessimistic scenarios. Joel Fetzer's investigation of the effects of unrestricted immigration through natural experiments in Miami, Marseille, and Dublin did reveal some negative effects such as overcrowding in housing and schools (which dissipated over time), as well as, more alarmingly, an increase in burglaries. Nonetheless, he concludes that the evidence suggests that most of the effects of large-scale immigration are manageable (Fetzer 2016). Hein de Haas, Simona Vezzoli, and María Villares-Varela's study of the effects of liberalizing border regimes in the EU concludes that initial migration surge in response to opening borders quickly subsides and is replaced by circular patterns of migration (Haas, Vezzoli, and Villares Varela 2019).

What would it take to achieve open borders? Imagine an updated North American Trade Agreement in which parties decide to negotiate migration. Mexican demographics have shifted and mass Mexican emigration to the United States has ended (Cornelius 2018). The manufactured Central American migration crisis has abated and mechanisms are in place to fairly and efficiently assess asylum applications and to welcome refugees. Negotiators recognize the perversity of the free trade of goods with rigid labor markets, as well as the moral and fiduciary costs of border enforcement. Moreover, activists have effectively communicated the brutality and racism of immigration controls, gaining significant public support.

The United States, Canada, and Mexico agree to phase-in a free movement for North America over a five-year period, gradually expanding the number of temporary visas available until nationals from any of the three countries can travel freely throughout the continent and apply for work permits. The temporary work permit application is not onerous—it is similar to applying for a driver's license—and can easily be converted to permanent residence after two years and to citizenship (if desired) after five years.

Of course, achieving open borders for the world would be much more difficult than the EU's achievement or my imagined North American free movement zone. We cannot be complacent about achievements that secure greater human freedom and equality. The imposition of internal border controls in Europe and Brexit is an example of ways in which openness can be reversed. The feasibility of progressive political proposals depends on the willingness to advocate for them. Their stability depends on continued vigilance and the refusal of complacency. Even if there are prospects for regional agreements allowing for open borders, this is quite different from free movement for the whole world. The trade-off for mobility within the Schengen area has been "Fortress Europe's" harsh, militarized policing of non-Europeans (De Genova 2017).

The same, though, can be said about any ambitious vision. It is easier to imagine the virtual elimination of extreme poverty in a particular region than worldwide. Nonetheless, the difficulty of bringing an end to poverty is no reason to deny it is possible. We should not confuse feasibility with inevitability or even a high likelihood. Many feasible goals are hard to achieve.

It is easier to argue for open borders as a moral ideal and to remain neutral about the prospects of achieving an open-bordered world. Nonetheless, optimism about realizing open borders has practical implications. Political activists and humanitarian actors often find themselves in a bind when deciding how to act. Progressive politicians may negotiate to legalize some immigrants at the price of increased border controls and the creation of "deserving" and "undeserving" categories of immigrants that feed xenophobic propaganda. Activists may advocate for keeping children out of immigrant detention without realizing that this contributes to the perpetuation of the myth that other detainees deserve their incarceration. Or they may contribute to releasing refugees into the community with tracking devices, stigmatizing their search for asylum.

People striving for migration justice need to decide what this entails. If the arguments of this monograph are persuasive, immigration enforcement raises grave issues of injustice. It curtails human freedom, perpetuates inequalities, upholds structural racism, and brutalizes millions of migrants merely because they happened to be born in another country. Activists need to decide what they will strive for. They need to ask if local victories are likely to support wider and more ambitious movements or if meeting their demands will merely allow authorities to legitimize oppression to the larger public. Service-providing agencies need to make a decision: should they provide needed services for incarcerated immigrants, even if this risks legitimizing detention? Scholars need to determine where to focus their research and how to communicate its results.

There are no easy answers to these questions and a variety of strategies from different actors are no doubt appropriate. Nonetheless, the acknowledgment that more radical alternatives are possible forces us to confront these questions directly. The insistence that open borders are infeasible gives us an easy way out: we should aim at immediate goals that have the highest probability of success. The danger of this is that success may foreclose more far-reaching reform by legitimizing and reinforcing unjust institutions. If open borders are at best a possibility for a very different society in a far-off future, then there is little point in trying to bring them about. I began this book with the example of Cédrik Herrou, who defied French law to assist refugees. In the United States, many communities of faith resist deportations by offering sanctuary in their buildings. If the arguments supporting open borders are correct, immigration laws violate basic freedoms and play a major role in imposing an unjust economic regime on much of the world. What follows? What is the connection between open borders as an ethical stance and political action?

Do migrants have a right to resist immigration controls? Are there obligations for bystanders to oppose unjust immigration laws? What means of opposition are acceptable? The next chapter turns to these questions.

NOTES

1. Passport Index, Global Passport Power Rank, https://www.passportindex.org/byRank.php

2. For critical discussion, see Dossa (2005) and Volpp (2001).

3. Thanks to Jonathan Echeverri Zuluaga for drawing my attention to this law.

4. Thanks to Robert Vinten for this point.

5. I have benefited here from Oliviero Angeli's valuable overview of this literature on Twitter: https://twitter.com/AngeliOliviero/status/1096421840631795714.

Chapter 7

Resistance and Refusal
(or Toward a World of Open Borders)

On July 12, 2019, around 700 illegalized migrant workers from the collective the *gilets noirs* (black vests) occupied the Panthéon. It was their third high-profile protest in less than two months. In May, they took over a wing of the Charles De Gaulle airport to protest Air France and its role in deporting migrants for the French State. In June, they occupied the catering multinational Elior to protest the treatment of their illegalized employees. In the Panthéon, they turned their attention to the French State, standing beneath the words "Live Free or Die" (*Vivre libre ou mourir*) on the pedestal of the monument of Marianne, personification of the republic. The leaflets they handed out explained:

> We are the undocumented, voiceless, faceless for the French republic. We come to the graves of your great citizens to denounce your irreverence [and] . . . to demand the Prime Minister give papers to all undocumented migrants in France. (Butterfly 2019)

The *gilets noirs* are one of many groups of migrants around the world who resist border controls, often at considerable personal risk and struggle to legalize migrants' status. The group takes their name from the *gilets jaunes* (yellow vests) movement against neoliberal austerity. But unlike the *gilets jaunes*, who distinguish themselves with their yellow vests, the *gilets noirs* proclaim that their vest is their face, calling out the hypocrisy and racism of the nation of *liberté, égalité*, and *fraternité* (Mathieu and Sall 2019).

The *gilets noirs* resist the unjust migration regimes of France and the EU, regimes that carry out deadly enforcement across the Mediterranean, incarcerate asylum seekers, outsource migration control to private companies and to foreign militia, and uphold racist and racialized subordination of immigrants in Europe. If the case for open borders is sound, immigration restrictions are grave injustices that should be restricted. Nonetheless, injustice alone does not settle the question of how to respond. A common conviction is that there is a *prima facie* obligation to obey the law. Some unjust laws should be obeyed and contested through established channels such as lobbying, voting, and authorized protest. Are immigration laws of this sort? If not, what measures are permissible or, possibly, required to resist them? Are migrants justified in crossing borders illegally? Are third parties morally wrong to smuggle migrants, either for humanitarian reasons or for financial gain? Who has a right and, possibly, a duty to resist unjust borders? What responsibilities do citizens living in states with unjust immigration laws have?

In this chapter, I give two grounds for resistance. First, there are the harms that immigration controls inflict on individual migrants. In the most extreme cases, immigration laws prevent immigrants from meeting their basic needs of food, shelter, and safety. In many other cases, immigration laws unjustly make people worse off than they would otherwise be by interfering with their ability to access opportunities. Because of these harms, migrants who peacefully violate many immigration laws are not committing injustice. Second, immigration restrictions as part of a larger system of oppression are an example of structural injustice that migrants have a right to resist. Moreover, most of us are to some degree complicit in this system, so we have obligations to take measures to dismantle it.

MIGRANTS: RESISTING INJUSTICE AND ACTS OF CITIZENSHIP

Oscar Martínez reports from his journey on the migrant trail from Mexico to the United States:

> The Ixtepec rail lights fade into the distance. We cut through dark plains outside of town, which glimmer in the eerie light of the yellow full moon.
>
> These are the migrants riding third class, those without either a coyote or money for a bus. The men repeat this fact over and over. They will be sleeping alongside these rails for the bulk of the trip across Mexico, hoping that as they rest they won't miss the next whistle and have to wait as long as three days for another train. They'll travel in these conditions for over 3,000 miles. This is The Beast, the snake, the machine, the monster. (Martínez 2013: 53)

The train is called The Beast because some migrants will fall onto the tracks and the train will sever their limbs or crush their skulls. If they survive the train, they may be robbed, raped, kidnapped, or murdered by police, soldiers, narcos, smugglers, or fellow migrants (categories that are not necessarily mutually exclusive). If they survive the migrant trail, they face *la migra* and the threat of detention and deportation in the United States.

Some of the migrants are motivated by poverty, others to join family. Still others travel not because they want to go to the United States but because of the threat of death from gangs or because of environmental degradation at home. In doing so, they violate immigration laws that Mexico and the United States vigorously and violently enforce. Are these violations justified? David Miller, reflecting on men trying to cross to the Spanish city of Melilla in North Africa, denies this:

> Surely, [these young African men] must understand that this is not the way to get into Europe. What clearer indication could there be of the proposition that illegal immigrants are not welcome than a double fence up to six meters tall with rolls of razor wire along the top? Do they think they have some kind of natural right to enter Spain in defiance of the laws that apply to everyone else who might like to move there? . . . Although I can understand their plight, which must indeed be desperate if they are willing to try, time and again, to risk life and limb to get across the border, I also think they are deluded and are responsible for their delusion. (Miller 2007: 3–4; for discussion, see Blunt 2018; Cabrera 2009; and Sager 2012a)

Miller is wrong; many migrants—including the young men attempting to crossing into Melilla—have a right to violate immigration laws. One way of justifying this right is to appeal to the right of necessity (Mancilla 2016). Alejandra Mancilla revives medieval and natural law conceptions of a right of necessity based on the right to subsistence. Rather than portraying the poor as passive recipients needing aid, she draws attention to their agency and asks what they are permitted to do. In circumstances of extreme need, the poor have a right to take other people's property to survive; property owners have a corresponding duty to allow them to do this (Mancilla 2016: 5). Migrants escaping poverty or environmental degradation can be seen as exercising their right of necessity, so many of the people riding The Beast through Mexico or seeking asylum in Melilla would be justified in violating Mexican, United States, and Spanish immigration laws (Mancilla 2016: 113).

Gwilym David Blunt provides a complementary analysis of severely impoverished migrants' right to resistance, which he compares to the rights of fugitive slaves to escape in the Antebellum United States. Blunt grounds this comparison on an analysis of systemic domination in which people's status "is arbitrarily determined by a social institution over which they have no control" (Blunt 2018: 90). He holds that the global poor are systemically dominated because the international system determines their status without giving them an opportunity to contest it. People suffering domination do not have secure access to their human rights; they are entitled to secure these rights through migration which Blunt deems an "example of infrapolitical resistance by severely dominated agents" (Blunt 2018: 83). Clandestine migration, in Blunt's analysis, can be a form of "infrapolitics," a term coined by James C. Scott to describe techniques that Southeastern Asian peasants use to resist oppression (Scott 1987; 1990). Since the authoritarian Malaysian government did not allow these peasants to openly protest or to access electoral politics, they turned to infrapolitical techniques such as tax evasion. Other infrapolitical techniques such as poaching, work slowdowns, petty theft, and informal boycotts can have far-reaching consequences, in some cases overturning unpopular policies. Clandestine immigration can be viewed as an infrapolitical rejection of the legitimacy of immigration controls. Immigrants crossing borders assert themselves as part of the community, even if they are exploited and marginalized members. It's for this reason that many no-borders activists see illicit migration as a form of protest and resistance, revealing the limitations of state power (King 2016). And despite rhetoric to the contrary, many states turn to legalization as a response to large numbers of illegalized migrants (Rosenblum 2010).

Mancilla and Blunt provide compelling reasons for holding that many migrants have a right to violate immigration laws, but their accounts have two limitations. First, they apply only to people unable to meet their basic needs. Migrants who are not severely impoverished do not appear to have a right to violate immigration laws. These include migrants seeking family-reunification and, possibly, even asylum seekers whose primary fear is state persecution or generalized violence. A second limitation in their accounts is that illicitly crossing borders is only one form of resistance. Infrapolitical resistance does not characterize the actions of groups like the *gilets noirs* or the Dreamers in the United States who openly confront state injustice.

To address the first limitation, we should expand the scope of migrants permitted to violate immigration laws. Javier Hidalgo provides a general defense of resistance, focusing not on subsistence rights but on unjust immigration restrictions. Hidalgo takes as an axiom that some immigration restrictions are unjust. Furthermore, border agents harm migrants by preventing them from crossing borders through force or through the threat of force. At the very least, migrants are unjustly harmed because they are unable to access opportunities. In his view, it is permissible for people to resist unjustified threats of harm through evasion, deception, and, even, defensive force when it is proportionate and necessary (Hidalgo 2015: 9). If the arguments for open borders in this book are cogent, immigration restrictions are unjust and there is a general right for immigrants to resist them.

I accept these arguments but think we need to also see migrants' resistance not merely as a response to individual harms or individual rights violations.

Migrants resisting borders are doing more than attempting to meet their basic needs or to protect their human rights. They are contesting an unjust migration regime embedded in nation-states, international law, and international organizations. The *gilets noirs* and the Dreamers openly confront unjust migration regimes and demand their inclusion. The protests are better understood as "acts of citizenship" (Isin and Nielsen 2008) in which migrants assert their belonging to the communities that exclude them. Many of these migrants are protesting an unjust system that categorizes them as unequal and inferior. To capture these types of protests, Peter Nyers draws on Bonnie Honig's account of politics, which, in turn, is influenced by Jacques Rancière's analysis of equality (Honig 2003; Rancière 1999). For Rancière, equality is not an ideal that politics should strive to implement; instead, equality is something that is enacted in practice when people who are denied equality insist on it. This occurs when "abject subjects"—those excluded from the official social order such as illegalized immigrants—"articulate a grievance as an equal speaking being" (Nyers 2003: 1078). Migrant protests can thus be conceived as a cosmopolitan movement to reshape and enlarge the political community by asserting belonging and equality (Sager 2018b). We should not conceive of these migrant protests primarily in terms of asserting individual rights, though they may do this as well. Instead, they serve an inclusive vision in which slogans such as "papers for all," "no one is illegal," or "undocumented and unafraid" seek to abolish the divisions between indigenous and immigrant.

Migrants have a right to resist immigration restrictions, either clandestinely or openly. But migration justice cannot only be the responsibility of migrants. If migrants are acting justly, there is at the very least an obligation not to interfere. In fact, the obligations of nonmigrants are more stringent. Affluent people around the world benefit from immigration laws that impose categorical inequalities that oppress and exploit migrants. In other words, they are complacent about their role in structural injustice. How, then, should nonmigrants respond to immigration laws and enforcement? Is noninterference with migrants asserting their rights against unjust laws sufficient or is there an obligation to assist them? What sorts of measures are permissible or required? Do citizens in countries with unjust immigration laws have an obligation to contact political representatives demanding reform? Should or must they participate in authorized protests, civil disobedience, or direct action? The next section turns to these questions.

THE RESPONSIBILITIES OF NONMIGRANTS

The US sanctuary movement arose in the 1980s as a response to refugees fleeing US-sponsored civil wars in Guatemala, Nicaragua, and El Salvador. Instead of allowing people fleeing death squads to apply for asylum or providing them with temporary membership, the Immigration and Naturalization Service decreed them "economic migrants" and targeted them for arrest and deportation (Gzesh 2006). When many US religious leaders and their congregations offered refugees sanctuary in their churches, the government prosecuted them for harboring "illegal aliens" (Pirie 1990: 383). For some congregations, the sanctuary movement for Central American refugees turned into a broader immigrant rights movement. Father Luis Olivares, a central figure in the Los Angeles sanctuary movement, responded to the Immigration Reform and Control Act (1986) by expanding sanctuary to include illegalized immigrants:

> The Lord's command is clear. In the book of Leviticus, God says, "When aliens reside with you in your land . . . you shall treat them no differently than the natives born among you." In the light of the Gospel's call to justice, we find ourselves unable to comply with the current regulations regarding the hiring of un-documented workers. Today, we stand with these people. . . . Therefore, we commit our-selves: To hire workers regardless of their legal status. To seek employment for non-qualifying workers by encouraging employers to hire the undocumented. To feed, clothe and house those rejected by the law. To call on other congregations and church leaders to respond in similar ways. We challenge the American people to acknowledge that the law, itself, is in violation of human rights, and we encourage them to respond to the needs of the undocumented with justice and compassion. (Cited in García 2018: 349)

The passage from *Leviticus* (33–4) continues its edict of open borders by instructing us to love the foreigner as we love ourselves.

Faith-based groups are at the core of the immigrant rights movement in the United States, allying with migrants by offering sanctuary as well as through political agitation and civil disobedience. Religious principles of hospitality and natural law have secular analogs in the principles of moral equality, freedom, antiracism, and anti-oppression defended in this book. Do these principles justify the actions of people such as Cédrik Herrou, who smuggled migrants across the French-Italian border; Danish activists Lisbeth Zornig and Mikael Lindholm, prosecuted for giving Syrian refugees a ride from Southern Denmark to Copenhagen; or Scott Warren, charged with harboring migrants as he provided humanitarian aid to people funneled by the US government through the Arizona desert? How should we conceive of the Stansted 15's locking themselves to a Boeing 767 set to deport refugees to Ghana, Nigeria, and Sierra Leone?

Herrou, Zornig, Lindholm, Warren, and the Stansted 15 are justified in resisting injustice.

It may be too demanding to insist that people risk incarceration at the frontlines of immigrant rights struggles. Nonetheless, citizens of democratic countries with unjust immigration laws are participating in upholding and benefiting from unjust institutions and are thus implicated in wrongdoing. They have a moral responsibility to contest these laws through established political channels. They also have more direct obligations to change unjust immigration laws and to abolish institutions that oppress migrants.

I follow Candice Delmas in arguing that people have a political obligation to resist injustice. When confronted with structural injustices such as those imposed by the institutions governing migration, there is an obligation to resist injustice which "involves refusing to cooperate with the mechanisms that produce and sustain it" (Delmas 2018: 16). This may involve civil disobedience—understood as "a conscientious, public, nonviolent breach of law undertaken to persuade the majority to change a law or policy in a nearly just society" (Delmas 2016: 25; cf. Rawls 1999: 320). Civil disobedience is a legitimate technique that migrants and their allies employ in immigrant rights movements, but it is a strategy that comes most easily for those who do not face deportation with arrest. Moreover, our states' actual migration regimes are far from nearly just. For these reasons, uncivil disobedience is also justified, "including political riots, vigilante self-defence, whistleblowing, sanctuary assistance, and graffiti street art" (Delmas 2018: 48).

Active resistance is important, but we should not lose sight of how migration injustice is sustained through the collusion of hundreds of millions of people. Many people directly participate in and benefit from immigration enforcement; in doing so, they incur a moral obligation to contest its wrongs. Consider this Border Patrol agent assigned to the detention center in McAllen Texas:

> "What happened to me in Texas is that I realized I had walled off my emotions so I could do my job without getting hurt," he said. "I'd see kids crying because they want to see their dads, and I couldn't console them because I had 500 to 600 other kids to watch over and make sure they're not getting in trouble. All I could do was make sure they're physically OK. I couldn't let them see their fathers because that was against the rules.
>
> "I might not like the rules," he added. "I might think that what we're doing wasn't the correct way to hold children. But what was I going to do? Walk away? What difference would that make to anyone's life but mine?"
>
> When asked whether he simply stopped caring, he said: "Exactly, to a point that's kind of dangerous. But once you do, you feel better." (Thompson 2019)

The unnamed Border Patrol agent exemplifies Hannah Arendt's phrase about the banality of evil (Arendt 2006). Most Border Patrol agents appear drawn to the job because of its decent wages, health care, and pensions and not because of any animus toward migrants. Many agents are of Hispanic descent and in some respects identify with the people they detain and deport (Cortez

2019). None of this justifies continuing to accept payment to work as a prison guard for migrant children—evil's banality doesn't make it any less evil. The agent's moral imagination fails him when he answers his question about what he should have done with a rhetorical question suggesting that walking away wouldn't make a difference in anyone's life but his own. He does not grapple with how the rationalizations of tens of thousands of people like him make the evil of his organization possible.

People working for agencies such as the Border Patrol or ICE have the most direct role in perpetrating injustice against migrants, but their work is sustained by many other people. In many places, government authorities co-opt employers, landlords, schools, health providers, and other organizations into immigration enforcement. When she was Home Secretary in 2012, Theresa May described her "hostile environment":

> "The aim is to create here in Britain a really hostile environment for illegal migration," [May] declares.
>
> Work is under way to deny illegal immigrants access to work, housing and services, even bank accounts. "What we don't want is a situation where people think that they can come here and overstay because they're able to access everything they need," she says.
>
> HM Revenue and Customs is coming down hard on companies that employ illegal immigrants, the Department of Work and Pensions is taking a "zero tolerance" approach to benefits claims, and local councils are closing impromptu shelters offering "beds in sheds," she says. (Kirkup and Winnett 2012)

The hostile environment strategic culminated in the Windrush Scandal in which thousands of people from the British Commonwealth and former colonies who arrived before 1973 were denied benefits and health care, lost their jobs or homes, and, in some cases, were detained and/or deported by the Home Office (Elgot 2018; Guardian Staff 2018). It is easy—and appropriate—to blame May for her role in this obscenity, but it overlooks how many more people are culpable. Delmas suggests that we have political obligations to "directly disobey laws that require reporting or prohibit assisting undocumented migrants" (Delmas 2018: 19). Healthcare providers, teachers, landlords, employers, and others who are asked to participate in immigration enforcement can refuse or at least protest and try to influence their organizations' policy. The silence of privileged people implicated in injustice is complicity.

The "hostile environment" in the United Kingdom and "attrition through enforcement" in the United States that encourage illegalized immigrants to "self-deport" alert us to another obligation. These policies depend on ideology, including a willingness to dehumanize and demonize migrants. They are built on the assumption that it is legitimate to inflict harm on immigrants, to detain and deport them, or to separate them from their spouses and children and parents. They assume that immigrants are not moral equals. They are only possible if a majority of people support or are at least willing to tolerate the human cost.

Citizens—including those disinclined to participate in protests or direct action—have an obligation to inform themselves about injustice carried out in their name. Once informed, they should communicate these injustices to their families, coworkers, and community members. Much of the discussions of immigration in politics and the media are fact-free and racist. People have an obligation to learn the facts and expose racism. They also have an obligation to contact their representatives and work at a local level to protect immigrant rights by demanding that local police, courts, schools, healthcare providers, and businesses do not cooperate with immigration enforcement. Finally, they should act in solidarity with immigrants, participating in migrant-led movements as allies.

MEDIA AND SCHOLARS

Last, we come to those who have the privilege of researching and reporting on migration. In a pair of columns for *The New York Times*'s The Ethicist, Anthony Appiah argued in favor of reporting a green-card marriage and for the permissibility reporting one's neighbor's care worker to ICE (Appiah 2015; 2017, discussed in Bertram 2017 and Hidalgo 2018). Appiah's view rests on his conviction that immigration laws are just, as well as the questionable belief that immigrants are "queue jumpers" (Hidalgo 2018: 161–62). Appiah's position is disconcerting, in part because, in other contexts, he is a subtle, cosmopolitan thinker. His claim that illegalized immigrants are "queue jumpers" was misinformed—there was no "queue" for most immigrants to "jump." As a political philosopher, he must have been aware of the complex debates in his field about the justice of immigration laws. Appiah failed as a scholar by giving a simplistic analysis that feeds into narratives of immigrants breaking laws and faking relationships to cheat a fair system. Sharing his opinion in the guise of a moral authority to a large audience without properly considering the implications was ethically irresponsible.

Everyone who writes about migration chooses how they portray migrants, what stories they tell, how they tell them, and who gets to tell them. They do so in a context in which well-funded anti-immigrant organizations such as the Center for Immigration Studies promote their own exclusionary narratives, publishing "research" designed to legitimate their ugly ideology and engaging in media campaigns to disguise their xenophobia with the "legitimate" concerns about the jobs or wages of vulnerable co-nationals, about the environment, or about liberal values. This creates ethical responsibilities to participate in resistance to unjust migration regimes by exposing the ideology that supports them.

Researchers and reporters are irresponsible when they reproduce narratives that harm immigrants. They need to be vigilant, alerting their audience when cynical politicians use immigrants as scapegoats and when stereotypes demonize groups of people. This means eschewing facile "neutrality" that attempts to give equal voice to all sides even when one side is motivated by xenophobia and racism. Moreover, the terms "immigrant," "migrant," or "refugee" can let us forget that everyone labeled by these categories is a person. This also means grappling with the ethics of displaying the drowned body of the three-year-old Syrian child Alan Kurdi or of the bodies of Óscar Alberto Martínez Ramírez and his toddler daughter, Valeria, on the banks of the Rio Grande (Chapell 2019; Durham 2018).

Against cynical efforts to dehumanize migrants, people representing migrants need to insist on migrants' humanity and to hear their voices. Gabriella Sanchez warns us that stories on human smuggling often "constitute yet another round of repetitive, palatable stories reducing women's experiences on the migration pathway to sex, suffering and subjugation" (Sanchez 2019: 33). In these stories, the women themselves are erased, replaced with faceless, passive victims in need of rescue. This feeds into a harmful, anti-trafficking narrative that justifies the militarization of borders and the criminalization of migration, compounding migrants' vulnerability (Sharma 2005).

Indeed, people across the political spectrum are too eager to feed narratives of crisis (Sager 2018a; Sager Forthcoming). This is true of immigration restrictionists who use fear to recruit support for enforcement, but it is also a danger for people who support migrants. We are bombarded by claims about unprecedented numbers of refugees and internally displaced people and apocalyptic predictions about how hundreds of millions of people will be driven from their homes because of environmental collapse (Bettini 2013). These claims are meant to attract support for humanitarian movements, but, in practice, they often overwhelm and numb people. Rather than soberly describing the real harms of forced displacement—often because of the foreign policy and economic expansion of affluent states—these narratives frame migration as out of control. They obscure how so many migration crises are manufactured, the result of deliberate state policies, including restrictive border controls that turn a normal human response—migration—into a crisis by curtailing it.

When writing on migration, we participate in the social construction of immigrants. Depending on what we write, we either legitimize the current system of immigration controls or resist it by challenging the ideas that support it. The legitimacy of immigration enforcement gains its support from cognitive biases such as methodological nationalism that falsely imagines nation-states as autonomous, homogenous containers. It is also the result of a failure to explore the implications of principles of freedom and equality, to oppose systems of oppression and exploitation, and to acknowledge the suffering inflicted by immigration enforcement. This book has been an extended argument that justice demands abolishing migration regimes that restrict movement and moving toward open borders. As such, it should be understood as a small effort to resist injustice and to contribute to social movements calling for open borders.

CONCLUSION

In September 1939, the French authorities detained the ailing, Jewish philosopher Walter Benjamin in the Stade de Colombes, along with other German and Austrian residents detained on the grounds that they might pose a threat to the French State. Benjamin was then transferred to an internment camp at the Château de Vernuche in Burgundy, where he remained until his liberation two months later, obtained through the intervention of PEN (the worldwide association of writers). He returned to Paris, only to flee again, on June 14, 1940, to Lourdes. On July 10, the French and German governments negotiated the end of the Third Republic.

Terrified of reinternment under the Vichy Regime, Benjamin secured a safe-conduct pass and departed for Marseilles. At the Marseille consulate, he received an entry visa for the United States, as well as transit visas for Spain and Portugal. He did not, however, obtain a visa to exit France. As the Vichy Regime published lists of German Jews and delivered anti-fascists to the Gestapo, Benjamin traveled by train from Marseille and embarked on a grueling journey through the Pyrenees. He reported to the Spanish customs office in the fishing village of Portbou, only to discover that the Spanish government had closed the border to refugees from France. The refugees were confined to the hotel, Fonda de Francia, to await deportation. Fearing that the Spanish would turn the refugees over to the Nazis, Benjamin wrote a note for his companion Henny Gurland:

> In a situation presenting no way out, I have no other choice but to make an end of it. It is in a small village in the Pyrenees, where no one knows me, that my life will come to a close [*va s'achever*].
>
> I ask you to transmit my thoughts to my friend Adorno and to explain to him the situation in which I find myself. There is not enough time remaining for me to write all the letters I would like to write. (Eiland and Jennings 2014: 675)

That night he committed suicide by overdosing on morphine.

An informed observer of Europe's borders from September 27, 1940, the day Benjamin died, would likely have scoffed at the possibility that only seventeen years later workers in the European Economic Community would enjoy free movement under the Treaty of Rome. The observers would scarcely have predicted that the right to move and reside freely within the territory of EU Member States would be codified in Citizens' Rights Directive 2004/38/EC or that today these rights would by enjoyed by over 400 million people from the 26 members of the Schengen Agreement.

It would have been easier to confidently praise the European achievement of open borders before the June 23, 2016 referendum in which the United Kingdom voted to withdraw from the EU or before the recent successes of far-right nationalist parties across the continent. As I write this conclusion, European countries are erecting internal border controls and many people fear for the future of the Europe Union (Krastev 2017). In the United States, Donald Trump has proclaimed that he is a nationalist, opposing his nationalism to (supposedly) Radical Democrats who "want to turn back the clock. Restore the rule of corrupt, power-hungry globalists" (Forgey 2018). As his presidency progresses, the white nationalism of the administration has become increasingly obvious.

In more sober circles, liberal scholars such as Jill Lepore, Martha Nussbaum, and Yael Tamir have turned to liberal accounts of the nation-state as a response to neoliberal capitalism and the rise of ethnic and populist forms of nationalism (Lepore 2019; Nussbaum, Martha Craven 2019; Tamir 2019). Tamir claims that "democracy cannot be restored as a purely utilitarian project, only as a national one—as a framework that provides meaning and reasons for the mutual care and responsibility" (Tamir 2019: xvi). She pits global elites against the less well-off nationals who turn to "an aggressive, xenophobic type of nationalism" to express their demand for inclusion and fair treatment (Tamir 2019: 9). She repudiates far-right nationalism, but nonetheless calls for a revival of nationalism through nation-building narratives.

We are at a juncture in which we are forced to choose between openness and closeness. Many people want to close themselves off to the world. Some are motivated by fear or hatred, others by a lack of imagination or the conviction that we cannot aspire to anything better than liberal nationalism. Pessimism about open borders in the near future is understandable. Nonetheless, if the arguments of this book are sound, nationalism, however liberal, is not the solution. Indeed, a world conceived of fixed populations, each with a right to regulate membership largely at their own discretion is not compatible with justice.

Migration reminds us that our shared human heritage is the result of a history of crossing borders. Migration is a part of life, a normal response to what has always been a mobile world. Migrants embody our shared humanity, enlarging our horizons and enriching our communities, not because they are foreigners but because in important ways they are us. The distinction between indigenous and immigrant obscures far more than it reveals, hiding not only how people are connected but also how they mutually constitute each other. In a world where states police their borders, the relationship between indigenous and immigrant is often one of domination or exploitation. We need to remember that there is nothing inevitable about state borders, let alone policies that classify people as foreigners or strangers, denying their equal standing. Attention to these relations should bring people together with shared duties to abolish these distinctions and to move toward an open-bordered world.

Bibliography

Abascal, Maria, and Delia Baldassarri. 2015. "Love Thy Neighbor? Ethnoracial Diversity and Trust Reexamined." *American Journal of Sociology* 121 (3): 722–82.

Abizadeh, A. 2008. "Democratic Theory and Border Coercion: No Right to Unilaterally Control Your Own Borders." *Political Theory* 36 (1): 37–65. https://doi.org/10.1177/0090591707310090.

Abizadeh, A. 2010. "Democratic Legitimacy and State Coercion: A Reply to David Miller."*Political Theory* 38(1):121–30.https://doi.org/10.1177/0090591709348192.

Abou-Chadi, Tarik, and Werner Krause. 2018. "The Causal Effect of Radical Right Success on Mainstream Parties' Policy Positions: A Regression Discontinuity Approach." *British Journal of Political Science* (June): 1–19. https://doi.org/10.1017/S0007123418000029.

Acosta Arcarazo, Diego, and Andrew Geddes. 2014. "Transnational Diffusion or Different Models? Regional Approaches to Migration Governance in the European Union and Mercosur." *European Journal of Migration and Law* 16 (1): 19–44. https://doi.org/10.1163/15718166-00002047.

Acosta, Diego. 2016. "Free Movement in South America: The Emergence of an Alternative Model?" Migration Policy Institute. Last accessed November 2, 2019. http://www.migrationpolicy.org/article/free-movement-south-america-emergence-alternative-model.

Adamson, Fiona B. 2006. "Crossing Borders: International Migration and National Security." *International Security* 31 (1): 165–99.

Adelman, Robert, Lesley Williams Reid, Gail Markle, Saskia Weiss, and Charles Jaret. 2017. "Urban Crime Rates and the Changing Face of Immigration: Evidence across Four Decades." *Journal of Ethnicity in Criminal Justice* 15 (1): 52–77. https://doi.org/10.1080/15377938.2016.1261057.

Agier, Michel. 2008. *On the Margins of the World: The Refugee Experience Today.* English ed. Cambridge, UK; Malden, MA: Polity.

Agnew, John. 1994. "The Territorial Trap: The Geographical Assumptions of International Relations Theory." *Review of International Political Economy* 1 (1): 53–80.

Aja, Alan A., and Alejandra Marchevsky. March 17, 2017. "How Immigrants Became Criminals." *Boston Review*. https://bostonreview.net/politics/alan-j-aja-alejandra-marchevsky-how-immigrants-became-criminals.

Albahari, Maurizio. 2015. *Crimes of Peace: Mediterranean Migrations at the World's Deadliest Border*. Philadelphia: University of Pennsylvania Press.

Alesina, Alberto, Armando Miano, and Stefanie Stantcheva. 2018. "Immigration and Redistribution." w24733. Cambridge, MA: National Bureau of Economic Research. https://doi.org/10.3386/w24733.

Alexander, Amy C., and Christian Welzel. 2011. "Islam and Patriarchy: How Robust Is Muslim Support for Patriarchal Values?" *World Values Research* 4 (2): 40–70.

Altman, Andrew, and Christopher Heath Wellman. 2009. *A Liberal Theory of International Justice*. New York: Oxford University Press.

Alvarez, Priscilla. July 23, 2019. "35 Arrested in Trump-Touted ICE Operation That Targeted 2,000." *CNN*. https://www.cnn.com/2019/07/23/politics/ice-raids-35-arrests/index.html.

American Civil Liberties Union, National Immigrant Justice Center, and Detention Watch Network. 2016. "Fatal Neglect: How ICE Ignores Deaths in Detention February 2016." https://www.detentionwatchnetwork.org/sites/default/files/reports/Fatal%20Neglect%20ACLU-DWN-NIJC.pdf.

Amnesty International. 2016. "Euro Risks Fueling Horrific Abuse of Refugees and Migrants in Libya." https://www.amnesty.org/en/latest/news/2016/06/eu-risks-fuelling-horrific-abuse-of-refugees-and-migrants-in-libya/.

Anderson, Benedict. 2016. *Imagined Communities: Reflections on the Origin and Spread of Nationalism*. Revised edition. London New York: Verso.

Andersson, Ruben. 2014. *Illegality, Inc.: Clandestine Migration and the Business of Bordering Europe*. California Series in Public Anthropology 28. Oakland: University of California Press.

Anderson, Bridget, Nandita Sharma, and Cynthia Wright. 2009. "Editorial: Why No Borders?" *Refuge* 26 (2): 5–17.

Andersson, Ruben. 2016. "Europe's Failed 'Fight' against Irregular Migration: Ethnographic Notes on a Counterproductive Industry." *Journal of Ethnic and Migration Studies* 42 (7): 1055–75. https://doi.org/10.1080/1369183X.2016.1139446.

Andersson, Ruben, and David Keen. 2019. "Partners in Crime? The Impact of Europe's Outsourced Migration Controls on Peace, Stability and Rights." *Saferworld*. https://www.saferworld.org.uk/resources/publications/1217-partners-in-crime-theimpacts-of-europeas-outsourced-migration-controls-on-peace-stability-and-rights.

Andrews, Abigail. 2018. *Undocumented Politics: Place, Gender, and the Pathways of Mexican Migrants*. Oakland: University of California Press.

Angus, Ian, and Simon Butler. 2011. *Too Many People? Population, Immigration, and the Environmental Crisis*. Chicago, IL: [Minneapolis, MN]: Haymarket Books; Distributed by Consortium Book Sales and Distribution.

Appiah, Kwame Anthony. October 11, 2015. "Is My Neighbor Obliged to Report Me to Immigration?" *The New York Times*. https://www.nytimes.com/2015/10/11/magazine/is-my-neighbor-obliged-to-report-me-to-immigration.html.

Appiah, Kwame Anthony. January 25, 2017. "Should You Report a Green-Card Marriage?" *The New York Times*. https://www.nytimes.com/2017/01/25/magazine/should-you-report-a-green-card-marriage.html.

Arendt, Hannah. 1959. "On Humanity in Dark Times: Thoughts about Lessing." In *Men in Dark Times*, 3–31. New York: Harcourt.

Arendt, Hannah. 2006. *Eichmann in Jerusalem: A Report on the Banality of Evil*. Penguin Classics. New York: Penguin Books.

Associated Press. July 2, 2019. "Border Activist to Be Retried in Case on Aiding Migrants July 2, 2019." https://www.apnews.com/1033606cb9424c7fb6d12b3e54f38f1e.

Aviv, Rachel. April 4, 2016. "The Cost of Caring." *The New Yorker*. https://www.newyorker.com/magazine/2016/04/11/the-sacrifices-of-an-immigrant-caregiver.

Balderrama, Francisco E., and Raymond Rodriguez. 2006. *Decade of Betrayal: Mexican Repatriation in the 1930s*. Rev. ed. Albuquerque: University of New Mexico Press.

Balibar, Étienne. 2002. *Politics and the Other Scene*. London: Verso.

Barry, Brian. 1992. "The Quest for Consistency: A Sceptical View." In *Free Movement: Ethical Issues in the Transnational Migration of People and Money*, edited by Brian Barry and Robert E. Goodin. University Park: Pennsylvania State University Press.

Basok, Tanya. 2009. *Tortillas and Tomatoes Transmigrant Mexican Harvesters in Canada*. Montreal: McGill-Queen's University Press. http://site.ebrary.com/id/10119956.

Bauböck, Rainer. 2007. "Stakeholder Citizenship and Transnational Political Participation: A Normative Evaluation of External Voting." *Fordham Law Review* 75: 2393–447.

Bauder, Harald. 2014. "Why We Should Use the Term 'Illegalized' Refugee or Immigrant: A Commentary." *International Journal of Refugee Law* 26 (3): 327–32.

Bauder, Harald. 2015. "Perspectives of Open Borders and No Border." *Geography Compass* 9 (7): 395–405. https://doi.org/10.1111/gec3.12224.

Bauder, Harald. 2017. *Migration Borders Freedom*. Routledge Studies in Human Geography 63. London; New York: Routledge is an imprint of the Taylor & Francis Group, an Informa Business.

BBC. November 11, 2014. "EU 'Benefit Tourism' Court Ruling Is Common Sense, Says Cameron." https://www.bbc.com/news/uk-politics-30002138.

BBC. April 12, 2018. "BBC Defends Rivers of Blood Broadcast." https://www.bbc.com/news/uk-43745447.

Beck, Roy Howard. 1996. *The Case against Immigration: The Moral, Economic, Social, and Environmental Reasons for Reducing U.S. Immigration Back to Traditional Levels*. New York: W. W. Norton.

Beine, Michel, Fréderic Docquier, and Hillel Rapoport. 2008. "Brain Drain and Human Capital Formation in Developing Countries: Winners and Losers." *The Economic Journal* 118 (528): 631–52. https://doi.org/10.1111/j.1468-0297.2008.02135.x.

Benhabib, Seyla. 2004. "The Law of Peoples, Distributive Justice, and Migrations." *Fordham Law Review* 72 (5): 1761–87.

Berry, Mike, Inaki Garcia, and Kerry Moore. 2015. "Press Coverage of the Refugee and Migrant Crisis in the EU: A Content Analysis of Five European Countries." Cardiff, UK: Cardiff School of Journalism, Media and Cultural Studies. http://

www.unhcr.org/en-us/protection/operations/56bb369c9/press-coverage-refugee-migrant-crisis-eu-content-analysis-five-european.html.

Bertram, Chris. January 31, 2017. "Snitching on Those in Breach of Immigration Law." *Crooked Timber* (blog). http://crookedtimber.org/2017/01/31/snitching-on-those-in-breach-of-immigration-law/.

Bertram, Christopher. 2018. *Do States Have the Right to Exclude Immigrants? Political Theory Today*. Cambridge, UK; Medford, MA: Polity.

Bettini, Giovanni. 2013. "Climate Barbarians at the Gate? A Critique of Apocalyptic Narratives on 'Climate Refugees.'" *Geoforum* 45 (March): 63–72. https://doi.org/10.1016/j.geoforum.2012.09.009.

Bier, David. 2018. "U.S. Citizens Targeted by ICE: U.S. Citizens Targeted by Immigration and Customs Enforcement in Texas." Policy Brief 8. Cato Institute. https://www.cato.org/publications/immigration-research-policy-brief/us-citizens-targeted-ice-us-citizens-targeted.

Black, Richard, Nigel· W. Arnell, W. Neil Adger, David Thomas, and Andrew Geddes. 2013. "Migration, Immobility and Displacement Outcomes Following Extreme Events." *Environmental Science & Policy* 27 (March): S32–43. https://doi.org/10.1016/j.envsci.2012.09.001.

Blake, Michael. 2013a. "Immigration, Jurisdiction, and Exclusion." *Philosophy & Public Affairs* 41 (2): 103–30.

Blake, Michael. 2013b. "We Are All Cosmopolitans Now." In *Cosmopolitanism versus Non-Cosmopolitanism: Critiques, Defenses, Reconceptualizations*, edited by Gillian Brock, 35–54. Oxford: Oxford University Press.

Blake, Michael. 2014. "The Right to Exclude." *Critical Review of International Social and Political Philosophy* 17 (5): 521–37. https://doi.org/10.1080/13698230.2014.919056.

Blake, Michael, and Matthias Risse. 2009. "Immigration and Original Ownership of the Earth." *Notre Dame Journal of Law, Ethics, and Public Policy* 23 (1): 133–65.

Blitzer, Jonathan. April 2019. "How Climate Change Is Fuelling the U.S. Border Crisis." *The New Yorker*. https://www.newyorker.com/news/dispatch/how-climate-change-is-fuelling-the-us-border-crisis.

Bloom, Tendayi, Katherine Tonkiss, and Phillip Cole, eds. 2017. *Understanding Statelessness: Lives in Limbo*. Routledge Studies in Human Rights 4. Abingdon, Oxon; New York: Routledge.

Blunt, Gwilym David. 2018. "Illegal Immigration as Resistance to Global Poverty." *Raisons Politiques* 69 (1): 83–98. https://doi.org/10.3917/rai.069.0083.

Böhning, W. R., and M. L. Scholeter-Paredes. 1994. *Aid in Place of Migration: Selected Contributions to an ILO-UNHRC Meeting*. Geneva: International Labour Office.

Borjas, G. J. 2003. "The Labor Demand Curve Is Downward Sloping: Reexamining the Impact of Immigration on the Labor Market." *The Quarterly Journal of Economics* 118 (4): 1335–74. https://doi.org/10.1162/003355303322552810.

Borjas, George J. 2001. *Heaven's Door: Immigration Policy and the American Economy*. Princeton, NJ: Princeton University Press.

Borjas, George. 2015. "The Wage Impact of the Marielitos: A Reappraisal." w21588. Cambridge, MA: National Bureau of Economic Research. https://doi.org/10.3386/w21588

Brimelow, Peter. December 29, 1997. "Milton Friedman at 85." *Forbes*. https://www. forbes.com/forbes/1997/1229/6014052a.html#2ef3d93c75d8.

Brock, Gillian. 2009. *Global Justice: A Cosmopolitan Account*. Oxford; New York: Oxford University Press.

Brock, Gillian, and Michael Blake. 2015. *Debating Brain Drain: May Governments Restrict Emigration?* New York: Oxford University Press.

Brubaker, Rogers. 2002. "Ethnicity without Groups." *European Journal of Sociology* 43(2): 163–89. https://doi.org/10.1017/S0003975602001066.

Buchanan, Patrick J. 2002. *The Death of the West*. New York: St. Martin's Griffin.

Buchanan, Patrick J. 2006. *State of Emergency*. New York: St. Martin's Press.

Butterfly, Luke. July 15, 2019. "The Gilets Noirs Occupy the Panthéon." *Verso* (blog). https://www.versobooks.com/blogs/4379-the-gilets-noirs-occupy-the-pantheon.

Cabrera, Luis. 2009. "An Archaeology of Borders: Qualitative Political Theory as a Tool in Addressing Moral Distance." *Journal of Global Ethics* 5(2): 109–23.

Cafaro, Philip, and Winthrop Staples. 2009. "The Environmental Argument for Reducing Immigration to the United States." *The Journal of Social, Political, and Economic Studies* 34 (3): 290–317.

Cafaro, Philip. 2015. *How Many Is Too Many?: The Progressive Argument for Reducing Immigration into the United States*. Chicago; London: The University of Chicago Press.

Calavita, Kitty. 1992. *Inside the State*. New York: Routledge.

Caldwell, Christopher. 2010. *Reflections on the Revolution in Europe: Immigration, Islam and the West*. New York: Anchor Books.

Card, David. 1990. "The Impact of the Mariel Boatlift on the Miami Labor Market." *Industrial and Labor Relations Review* 43 (2): 245. https://doi.org/10.2307/2523702.

Card, David. 2005. "Is the New Immigration Really So Bad?" *The Economic Journal* 115(507): F300–323. https://doi.org/10.1111/j.1468-0297.2005.01037.x.

Carens, Joseph H. 1987. Aliens and Citizens: The Case for Open Borders. The Review of Politics 49(2), 251–73.

Carens, Joseph H. 1992. "Migration and Morality: A Liberal Egalitarian Perspective." In *Free Movement: Ethical Issues in the Transnational Migration of People and of Money*, 25–47. University Park: Pennsylvania State University Press.

Carens, Joseph H. 1996. "Realistic and Idealistic Approaches to the Ethics of Migration." *International Migration Review* 30 (1): 156–70. https://doi.org/10.2307/2547465.

Carens, Joseph H. 2000. "Open Borders and Liberal Limits: A Response to Isbister." *International Migration Review* 34 (2): 636–43. https://doi.org/10.1177/01979 1830003400232.

Carens, Joseph H. 2013. *The Ethics of Immigration*. New York: Oxford University Press.

Cartwright, Nancy, and Jacob Stegenga. 2011. "A Theory of Evidence for Evidence-Based Policy." *Proceedings of the British Academy* 171: 289–319.

Casey, John P. 2010. "Open Borders: Absurd Chimera or Inevitable Future Policy?: Open Borders: Chimera or Future Policy?" *International Migration* 48 (5): 14–62. https://doi.org/10.1111/j.1468-2435.2009.00514.x.

Castles, Stephen, Hein de Haas, and Mark J. Miller. 2014. *The Age of Migration: International Population Movements in the Modern World*. Fifth ed. New York: Guilford Press.

Cavallero, Eric. 2006. "An Immigration-Pressure Model of Global Distributive Justice." *Politics, Philosophy & Economics* 5 (1): 97–127.

Chacón, Jennifer M. 2012. "Overcriminalizing Immigration." *Journal of Criminal Law and Criminology* 102 (3): 613–65.

Chacón, Jennifer M. 2014. "Immigration Detention: No Turning Back?" *South Atlantic Quarterly* 621: 621–26.

Chamberlain, James A. 2017. "Minoritarian Democracy: The Democratic Case for No Borders." *Constellations* 24 (2): 142–53. https://doi.org/10.1111/1467-8675.12236.

Chandler, Caitlin L. January 30, 2018. "Inside the EU's Flawed $200 Million Migration Deal with Sudan." *The New Humanitarian.* https://www.thenewhumanitarian. org/special-report/2018/01/30/inside-eu-s-flawed-200-million-migration-deal-sudan.

Chang, Howard F. 2003. "The Immigration Paradox: Poverty, Distributive Justice, and Liberal Egalitarianism." *DePaul Law Review* 52: 759–76.

Chang, Howard F. 2007. "The Economic Impact of International Labor Migration: Recent Estimates and Policy Implications." *Temple Political & Civil Rights Law Review* 16: 321–33.

Chang, Howard F. 2008. "The Economics of International Labor Migration and the Case for Global Distributive Justice in Liberal Political Theory." *Cornell International Law Journal* 41: 1–25.

Chapell, Bill. June 26, 2019. "A Father and Daughter Who Drowned at the Border Put Attention on Immigration." *NPR.* https://www.npr.org/2019/06/26/736177694/ a-father-and-daughter-drowned-at-the-border-put-attention-on-immigration.

Chávez, Leo R. 2013. *The Latino Threat: Constructing Immigrants, Citizens, and the Nation.* Second ed. Stanford, CA: Stanford University Press.

Chishti, Muzaffar, Sarah Pierce, and Laura Plata. June 29, 2018. "In Upholding Travel Ban, Supreme Court Endorses Presidential Authority While Leaving Door Open for Future Challenges." *Migration Policy Institute.* https://www.migra tionpolicy.org/article/upholding-travel-ban-supreme-court-endorses-presidential-authority-while-leaving-door-open.

Clemens, Michael. 2016. "Losing Our Minds? New Research Directions on Skilled Emigration and Development." *International Journal of Manpower* 37(7): 1227–48. https://doi.org/10.1108/IJM-07-2015-0112.

Clemens, Michael A. 2011. "Economics and Emigration: Trillion-Dollar Bills on the Sidewalk?" *Journal of Economic Perspectives* 25(3): 83–106. https://doi.org/ 10.1257/jep.25.3.83.

Clemens, Michael, and Hannah Postel. February 12, 2018. "Deterring Emigration with Foreign Aid: An Overview of Evidence from Low-Income Countries." CGD Policy Paper 119. https://www.cgdev.org/sites/default/files/deterring-emigration-foreign-aid-overview-evidence-low-income-countries.pdf.

Clemens, Michael A., and Jennifer Hunt. 2019. "The Labor Market Effects of Refugee Waves: Reconciling Conflicting Results." *ILR Review* 72 (4): 818–57. https:// doi.org/10.1177/0019793918824597.

Clemens, Michael A., and Lant Pritchett. 2008. "Income per Natural: Measuring Development for People Rather Than Places." *Population and Development Review* 34(3): 395–434. https://doi.org/10.1111/j.1728-4457.2008.00230.x.

Clemens, Michael A., Claudio E. Montenegro, and Lant Pritchett. 2019. "The Place Premium: Bounding the Price Equivalent of Migration Barriers." *The Review of Economics and Statistics* 101 (2): 201–13. https://doi.org/10.1162/rest_a_00776.

Clifton, Jon. April 20, 2012. "150 Million Adults Worldwide Would Migrate to the U.S." *Gallup.* http://www.gallup.com/poll/153992/150-million-adults-worldwide-migrate.aspx.

Cohen, Elizabeth F. 2018. *The Political Value of Time: Citizenship, Duration and Democratic Justice.* Cambridge, UK; New York: Cambridge University Press.

Cohen, Robin. 2006. *Migration and Its Enemies: Global Capital, Migrant Labour, and the Nation State.* Burlington, VT: Ashgate Publishing Company.

Cole, Phillip. 2000. *Philosophies of Exclusion: Liberal Political Theory and Immigration.* Edinburgh: Edinburgh University Press.

Collier, Paul. 2013. *Exodus: How Migration Is Changing Our World.* Oxford: Oxford University Press.

Cornelius, Wayne A. 2001. "Death at the Border: Efficacy and Unintended Consequences of US Immigration Control Policy." *Population and Development Review* 27(4): 661–85.

Cornelius, Wayne. November 2018. "Mexico: From Country of Mass Emigration to Transit State." Inter-American Development Bank. https://doi.org/10.18235/0001415.

Cortez, David. 2019. "I Asked Latinos Why They Joined Immigration Law Enforcement. Now I'm Urging Them to Leave." USA Today, July 3, 2019. https://www.usatoday.com/story/opinion/voices/2019/07/03/latino-border-patrol-ice-agents-immigration-column/1619511001/.

Cortez, David. July 3, 2019. "I Asked Latinos Why They Joined Immigration Law Enforcement. Now I'm Urging Them to Leave." *USA Today.* https://www.usatoday.com/story/opinion/voices/2019/07/03/latino-border-patrol-ice-agents-immigration-column/1619511001/.

Coulter, Ann H. 2016. *Adios, America: The Left's Plan to Turn Our Country into a Third World Hellhole.* Washington, D.C.: Regnery Publishing.

Cowen, Tyler. 2007. "The Importance of Defining the Feasible Set." *Economics and Philosophy* 23(1): 1. https://doi.org/10.1017/S0266267107001198.

Cranston, Maurice. 1973. *What Are Human Rights?* London: The Bodley Head.

Dancygier, Rafaela M. 2010. *Immigration and Conflict in Europe.* New York: Cambridge Univ. Press.

Dauvergne, Catherine. 2008. *Making People Illegal: What Globalization Means for Migration and Law.* Cambridge, UK; New York: Cambridge University Press.

Dawsey, Josh. January 12, 2018. "Trump Derides Protections for Immigrants from 'Shithole' Countries." *Washington Post.* https://www.washingtonpost.com/politics/trump-attacks-protections-for-immigrants-from-shithole-countries-in-oval-office-meeting/2018/01/11/bfc0725c-f711–11e7–91af-31ac729add94_story.html?utm_term=.d399fcabd6fd.

De Genova, Nicholas P. 2002. "Migration 'Illegality' and Deportability in Everyday Life." *Annual Review of Anthropology* 31: 419–47.

De Genova, Nicholas. 2010. "The Deportation Regime: Sovereignty, Space, and the Freedom of Movement." In *The Deportation Regime: Sovereignty, Space, and the*

Freedom of Movement, edited by Nicholas De Genova and Nathalie Mae Peutz, 33–65. Durham, NC: Duke University Press.

De Genova, Nicholas. 2013. "Spectacles of Migrant 'Illegality': The Scene of Exclusion, the Obscene of Inclusion." *Ethnic and Racial Studies* 36(7): 1180–98. https://doi.org/10.1080/01419870.2013.783710.

De Genova, Nicholas, ed. 2017. *The Borders of "Europe": Autonomy of Migration, Tactics of Bordering*. Durham, NC: Duke University Press.

de León, Jason. 2015. *The Land of Open Graves: Living and Dying on the Migrant Trail*. California Series in Public Anthropology 36. Oakland: University of California Press.

Dearden, Lizzie. March 11, 2016. "Prominent Danish Activist and Author Prosecuted for 'People Trafficking' after Giving Syrian Refugee Family a Lift." *The Independent*. http://www.independent.co.uk/news/world/europe/prominent-danish-activist-and-author-lisbeth-zornig-prosecuted-for-people-trafficking-after-giving-a6925761.html.

Degler, Eva, and Thomas Liebig. 2017. "Finding Their Way: Labour Market Integration of Refugees in Germany." Organization for Economic Cooperation and Development. http://www.oecd.org/els/mig/Finding-their-Way-Germany.pdf.

Del Valle, Gaby. July 25, 2019. "U.S. Citizen Held by Border Patrol Says He Lost 26 Pounds and Couldn't Shower for 23 Days." *Vice*. https://news.vice.com/en_us/article/7xggy4/us-citizen-held-by-border-patrol-says-he-lost-26-pounds-and-couldnt-shower-for-23-days.

Delmas, Candice. 2018. *A Duty to Resist*. New York, N.Y.: Oxford University Press. https://doi.org/10.1093/oso/9780190872199.001.0001.

Devereaux, Ryan. June 12, 2019. "Felony Trial of No More Deaths Volunteer Scott Warren Ends in Mistrial." *The Intercept*. https://theintercept.com/2019/06/12/felony-trial-of-no-more-deaths-volunteer-scott-warren-ends-in-mistrial/.

Docquier, Frédéric, and Hillel Rapoport. 2012. "Globalization, Brain Drain, and Development." *Journal of Economic Literature* 50 (3): 681–730. https://doi.org/10.1257/jel.50.3.681.

Dossa, Shiraz. 2005. "Bad, Bad Multiculturalism!!" *The European Legacy* 10 (6): 641–44. https://doi.org/10.1080/10848770500254191.

Dowty, Alan. 1987. *Closed Borders: The Contemporary Assault on Freedom of Movement*. New Haven, CT; London: Yale University Press.

Dummett, Ann. 1992. "The Transnational Migration of People Seen from within a Natural Law Tradition." In *Free Movement: Ethical Issues in the Transnational Migration of People and of Money*, 169–80. University Park: The Pennsylvania State University Press.

Durham, Meenakshi Gigi. 2018. "Resignifying Alan Kurdi: News Photographs, Memes, and the Ethics of Embodied Vulnerability." *Critical Studies in Media Communication* 35 (3): 240–58. https://doi.org/10.1080/15295036.2017.1408958.

Echeverri Zuluaga, Jonathan, and Liza Acevedo Sáenz. 2018. "Pensando a Través de La Errancia: Travesías y Esperas de Viajeros Africanos En Quito y Dakar." *Antípoda Revista de Antropología y Arqueología* 32 (July): 105–23. https://doi.org/10.7440/antipoda32.2018.05.

Ehrlich, Paul Ralph. 1971. *The Population Bomb*. Cutchogue, NY: Buccaneer Books.
Ehrlich, Paul R., and Anne H. Ehrlich. 1991. *The Population Explosion*. New York: Simon & Schuster.
Eiland, Howard, and Michael William Jennings. 2014. *Walter Benjamin: A Critical Life*. Cambridge, MA: The Belknap Press of Harvard University Press.
Elgot, Jessica. April 17, 2018. "Theresa May's 'Hostile Environment' at Heart of Windrush Scandal." *The Guardian*. https://www.theguardian.com/uk-news/2018/apr/17/theresa-mays-hostile-environment-policy-at-heart-of-windrush-scandal.
Esipova, Neli, Julie Ray, Anita Pugliese, and Dato Tsabutashvil. 2015. "How the World Views Migration." Geneva, Switzerland: International Organization for Migration. http://publications.iom.int/system/files/how_the_world_gallup.pdf.
Esposito, John L., and Dalia Mogahed. 2007. *Who Speaks for Islam?: What a Billion Muslims Really Think*. New York: Gallup Press.
European Commission. 2014. "Labour Mobility within the EU." MEMO/14/541. Brussels. http://europa.eu/rapid/press-release_MEMO-14-541_en.htm.
Ewing, Walter, Daniel E. Martínez, and Rubén Rumbaut. 2015. "The Criminalization of Immigration in the United States." Special Report. American Immigration Council. https://www.americanimmigrationcouncil.org/research/criminalization-immigration-united-states.
Farley, Robert. July 3, 2018. "Calls to Abolish ICE Not 'Open Borders.'" *Factcheck. Org*. https://www.factcheck.org/2018/07/calls-to-abolish-ice-not-open-borders/.
Farrell, Paul, Nick Evershed, and Helen Davidson. August 10, 2016. "The Nauru Files: Cache of 2,000 Leaked Reports Reveal Scale of Abuse of Children in Australian Offshore Detention." *The Guardian*. https://www.theguardian.com/australia-news/2016/aug/10/the-nauru-files-2000-leaked-reports-reveal-scale-of-abuse-of-children-in-australian-offshore-detention.
Fernández-Reino, Mariña. 2019. "English Language Use and Proficiency of Migrants in the UK." Oxford: The Migration Observatory. https://migrationobservatory.ox.ac.uk/resources/briefings/english-language-use-and-proficiency-of-migrants-in-the-uk/.
Fetzer, Joel S. 2016. *Open Borders and International Migration Policy: The Effects of Unrestricted Immigration in the United States, France, and Ireland*. London: Palgrave Macmillan UK.
Fine, Sarah. 2017. "Migration, Political Philosophy, and the Real World." *Critical Review of International Social and Political Philosophy* 20(6): 719–25. https://doi.org/10.1080/13698230.2016.1231793.
Fisman, Raymond, and Edward Miguel. 2007. "Corruption, Norms, and Legal Enforcement: Evidence from Diplomatic Parking Tickets." *Journal of Political Economy* 115 (6): 1020–48. https://doi.org/10.1086/527495.
Fiss, Owen. October 1, 1998. "The Immigrant as Pariah." *Boston Review*. https://bostonreview.net/forum/owen-fiss-immigrant-pariah.
FitzGerald, David, and David Cook-Martín. 2014. *Culling the Masses: The Democratic Origins of Racist Immigration Policy in the Americas*. Cambridge, MA: Harvard University Press.
Flagg, Anna. 2018. "The Myth of the Criminal Immigrant by Anna Flagg." The Marshall Project. https://www.themarshallproject.org/2018/03/30/the-myth-of-the-criminal-immigrant.

Forgey, Quint. October 22, 2018. "Trump: 'I'm a Nationalist.'" *Politico*. https://www.politico.com/story/2018/10/22/trump-nationalist-926745.

Fourier, Charles. 1996. *The Theory of the Four Movements*, edited by Ian Patterson and Gareth Stedman Jones. Cambridge Texts in the History of Political Thought. Cambridge, UK; New York: Cambridge University Press.

Frankopan, Peter. 2016. *The Silk Roads: A New History of the World*. First US ed. New York: Alfred A. Knopf.

Freeman, Gary P. 2006. "National Models, Policy Types, and the Politics of Immigration in Liberal Democracies." *West European Politics* 29 (2): 227–47.

Freiman, Christopher, and Javier Hidalgo. 2016. "Liberalism or Immigration Restrictions, but Not Both." *Journal of Ethics and Social Philosophy* 12 (2): 1–20.

Frum, David. April 2019. "If Liberals Won't Enforce Borders, Fascists Will." *The Atlantic*. https://www.theatlantic.com/magazine/archive/2019/04/david-frum-how-much-immigration-is-too-much/583252/.

Gabaccia, Donna R. 2010. "Nations of Immigrants: Do Words Matter?" *The Pluralist* 5 (3): 5–31.

Galbraith, John Kenneth. 1979. *The Nature of Mass Poverty*. Cambridge, MA: Harvard University Press.

García Hernández, César Cuauhtémoc. 2013. "Creating Crimmigration." *Brigham Young University Law Review*, 1457–516.

García Hernández, César Cuauhtémoc. 2017. "Abolishing Immigration Prisons." *Boston University Law Review* 97: 245–300.

García, Mario T. 2018. *Father Luis Olivares, a Biography: Faith Politics and the Origins of the Sanctuary Movement in Los Angeles*. Chapel Hill: The University of North Carolina Press.

Gayle, Damien. February 6, 2019. "Stansted 15: No Jail for Activists Convicted of Terror-Related Offences." *The Guardian*. https://www.theguardian.com/global/2019/feb/06/stansted-15-rights-campaigners-urge-judge-to-show-leniency.

Gerstle, Gary. 2017. *American Crucible: Race and Nation in the Twentieth Century*. Princeton, New Jersey: Princeton University Press.

Gesthuizen, Maurice, Tom van der Meer, and Peer Scheepers. 2009. "Ethnic Diversity and Social Capital in Europe: Tests of Putnam's Thesis in European Countries." *Scandinavian Political Studies* 32 (2) (June): 121–42. https://doi.org/10.1111/j.1467-9477.2008.00217.x.

Gill, Nick. 2009. "Whose 'No Borders'? Achieving Border Liberalization for the Right Reasons." *Refuge* 26 (2): 107–20.

Gilabert, Pablo, and Holly Lawford-Smith. 2012. "Political Feasibility: A Conceptual Exploration." *Political Studies* 60 (4): 809–25. https://doi.org/10.1111/j.1467-9248.2011.00936.x.

Gleeson, Madeline. 2016. *Offshore: Behind the Wire on Manus and Nauru*. A NewSouth Book. Kensington, Australia: University of New South Wales.

Global Detention Project. 2019. "Global Detention Project Annual Report 2018." Special Reports. Global Detention Project. https://www.globaldetentionproject.org/global-detention-project-annual-report-2018.

Goldin, Ian, Geoffrey Cameron, and Meera Balarajan. 2011. *Exceptional People: How Migration Shaped Our World and Will Define Our Future.* Princeton, NJ: Princeton University Press.

Gomez, Alan. March 20, 2017. "Washington County No. 7 on Trump's 'Sanctuary City' Weekly List." *KGW News.* http://www.kgw.com/news/politics/president-trump-pressures-sanctuary-cities-that-wont-hold-undocumented-immigrants/423970366.

Gonzalez-Barrera, Ana, and Phillip Connor. March 14, 2019. "Around the World, More Say Immigrants Are a Strength than a Burden." Pew Research Center https://www.pewresearch.org/global/2019/03/14/around-the-world-more-say-immigrants-are-a-strength-than-a-burden/ [Last accessed November 3, 2019].

Government of Ecuador. 2017. "Ley Orgánica de La Movilidad Humana—Suplemento." Registro Oficial 938. https://www.acnur.org/fileadmin/Documentos/BDL/2017/10973.pdf.

Grande, Edgar, Tobias Schwarzbözl, and Matthias Fatke. 2018. "Politicizing Immigration in Western Europe." *Journal of European Public Policy* (October): 1–20. https://doi.org/10.1080/13501763.2018.1531909.

Grant, Madison. 1916. *The Passing of the Great Race: Or, The Racial Basis of European History.* New York, NY: Charles Scribner's Sons.

Greenhill, Kelly M. 2010. *Weapons of Mass Migration: Forced Displacement, Coercion, and Foreign Policy.* Cornell Studies in Security Affairs. Ithaca, NY: Cornell University Press.

Griffin, James. 2001. "Discrepancies between the Best Philosophical Account of Human Rights and the International Law of Human Rights." *Proceedings of the Aristotelian Society (Hardback)* 101 (1): 1–28. https://doi.org/10.1111/j.0066-7372.2003.00019.x.

Guardian Staff. April 20, 2018. "'It's Inhumane': The Windrush Victims Who Have Lost Jobs, Homes and Loved Ones." *The Guardian.* https://www.theguardian.com/uk-news/2018/apr/20/its-inhumane-the-windrush-victims-who-have-lost-jobs-homes-and-loved-ones.

Gzesh, Era. 2006. "Central Americans and Asylum Policy in the Reagan Era." Washington, D.C.: Migration Policy Institute. https://www.migrationpolicy.org/article/central-americans-and-asylum-policy-reagan-era.

Haas, Hein de. 2007a. "Turning the Tide? Why Development Will Not Stop Migration." *Development and Change* 38 (5): 819–41.

Haas, Hein de. 2007b. "Remittances, Migration, and Social Development: A Conceptual Review of the Literature." Social Policy and Development Program Paper Number 34, October, United Nations Research Institute for Social Development.

Haas, Hein de. 2008. "The Myth of Invasion: The Inconvenient Realities of African Migration to Europe." *Third World* 29 (7): 1305–22.

Haas, Hein de. 2012. "The Migration and Development Pendulum: A Critical View on Research and Policy." *International Migration* 50 (3): 8–25.

Haas, Hein de. August 29, 2016. "The Case for Border Controls." http://heindehaas.blogspot.com/2016/08/the-case-for-border-controls.html.

Haas, Hein de, Katharina Natter, and Simona Vezzoli. 2018. "Growing Restrictiveness or Changing Selection? The Nature and Evolution of Migration Policies 1."

International Migration Review 52 (2): 324–67. https://doi.org/10.1111/imre. 12288.

Haas, Hein de, Simona Vezzoli, and María Villares-Varel. 2019. "Opening the Floodgates? European Migration under Restrictive and Liberal Border Regimes 1950–2010." IMIn Working Paper Series 150. International Migration Institute Network.

Hacking, Ian. 2004. *Historical Ontology*. Harvard University Press paperback ed. Cambridge, MA: Harvard University Press.

Halliday, Josh, and Libby Brooks. July 5, 2019. "Johnson Pledges to Make All Immigrants Learn English." *The Guardian*. https://amp.theguardian.com/politics/2019/jul/05/johnson-pledges-to-make-all-immigrants-learn-english?CMP=share_btn_tw&__twitter_impression=true.

Hampshire, James. 2013. *The Politics of Immigration*. Malden, MA: Polity Press.

Hardin, Garrett. 1974. "Lifeboat Ethics: The Case against Helping the Poor." *Psychology Today*: 800–812.

Harris Poll. 2018. "Harvard Harris Poll: January 2018 Refield." http://harvardharris poll.com/wp-content/uploads/2018/01/Final_HHP_Jan2018-Refield_Registered-Voters_XTab.pdf.

Haslam, Nick, and Steve Loughnan. 2014. "Dehumanization and Infrahumanization." *Annual Review of Psychology* 65 (1): 399–423. doi:10.1146/annurev-psych-010213-115045.

Haslam, Nick, and Michelle Stratemeyer. 2016. "Recent Research on Dehumanization." *Current Opinion in Psychology* 11 (October): 25–29. https://doi.org/10.1016/j.copsyc.2016.03.009.

Hatton, Timothy J., and Jeffrey G. Williamson. 1998. *The Age of Mass Migration: Causes and Impact*. New York: Oxford University Press.

Hayek, Friedrich A. 1960. *The Constitution of Liberty*. Chicago: Univ. of Chicago Press.

Hernández, Kelly Lytle. 2010. *Migra! A History of the U.S. Border Patrol*. American Crossroads 29. Berkeley, Calif: University of California Press.

Hernández, Kelly Lytle. 2011. "Amnesty or Abolition?" *Boom: A Journal of California* 1 (4): 54–68. https://doi.org/10.1525/boom.2011.1.4.54.

Hernandez, Kelly Lytle. March 8, 2017. "Largest Deportation Campaign in US History Is No Match for Trump's Plan." *The Conversation*. http://bit.ly/2mjAVPy.

Heyman, Josiah McC. 1998. *Finding a Moral Heart for U.S. Immigration Policy*. Washington, D.C.: American Anthropological Association.

Heyman, Josiah McC. 2011. "The U.S. Political Community: Anti-Immigration Sentiment and Issues of Race, Class, Gender, Conscience, and Political Belief," edited by Kathleen R. Arnold. *Anti-Immigration in the United States: A Historical Encyclopedia*. Santa Barbara, CA: Greenwood.

Hidalgo, Javier S. 2012. "Freedom, Immigration, and Adequate Options." *Critical Review of International Social and Political Philosophy* (November): 1–23. https://doi.org/10.1080/13698230.2012.740178.

Hidalgo, Javier. 2015. "Resistance to Unjust Immigration Restrictions." *Journal of Political Philosophy* 23 (4): 450–70. https://doi.org/10.1111/jopp.12051.

Hidalgo, Javier S. 2016. "The Missing Evidence in Favour of Restricting Emigration." *Journal of Medical Ethics* (January) medethics-2015-103165. https://doi.org/10.1136/medethics-2015-103165.

Hidalgo, Javier S. 2018. *Unjust Borders: Individuals and the Ethics of Immigration.* First ed. New York, NY: Routledge. https://doi.org/10.4324/9781315145235.

Higgins, Peter. 2013. *Immigration Justice.* Edinburgh: Edinburgh University Press.

Hines, Annie Laurie, and Giovanni Peri. 2019. "Immigrants' Deportations, Local Crime and Police Effectiveness." IZA Discussion Paper 12413 http://ftp.iza.org/dp12413.pdf [Last accessed November 3, 2019].

Hing, Bill Ong. 2009. "Institutional Racism, ICE Raids, and Immigration Reform." *University of San Francisco Law Review* 44 (1): 1–49.

Hirota, Hidetaka. 2017. *Expelling the Poor: Atlantic Seaboard States and the Nineteenth-Century Origins of American Immigration Policy.* New York: Oxford University Press.

Hirschman, Albert O. 1978. "Exit, Voice, and the State." *World Politics* 31 (01): 90–107. https://doi.org/10.2307/2009968.

Hoerder, Dirk. 2011. *Cultures in Contact: World Migrations in the Second Millennium.* Paperback ed. Durham, NC: Duke University Press.

Hogan, Jackie, and Kristin Haltinner. 2015. "Floods, Invaders, and Parasites: Immigration Threat Narratives and Right-Wing Populism in the USA, UK and Australia." *Journal of Intercultural Studies* 36 (5): 520–43. https://doi.org/10.1080/0725 6868.2015.1072907.

Honig, Bonnie. 2003. *Democracy and the Foreigner.* Princeton, NJ: Princeton University Press.

https://papers.ssrn.com/sol3/papers.cfm?abstract_id=3408311.

Huemer, Michael. 2010. "Is There a Right to Immigrate?" *Social Theory and Practice* 36 (3): 429–61. doi:10.5840/soctheorpract201036323.

Hume, David. 2006. *An Enquiry Concerning the Principles of Morals: A Critical Edition*, edited by Tom L. Beauchamp. Oxford: Clarendon Press.

Human Rights First. 2012. "How to Repair the U.S. Immigration Detention System: Blueprint for the Next Administration." New York, NY and Washington, D.C.: Human Rights First. https://www.humanrightsfirst.org/wp-content/uploads/pdf/immigration_detention_blueprint.pdf.

Huntington, Samuel P. 2004. *Who Are We?: The Challenges to America's National Identity.* New York: Simon & Schuster.

International Organization for Migration. n.d. Missing Migrants' Project. https://missingmigrants.iom.int/

Iqbal, Nosheen. December 16, 2018. "Stansted 15: 'We Are Not Terrorists, No Lives Were at Risk. We Have No Regrets.'" *The Guardian* https://www.theguardian.com/world/2018/dec/16/migrants-deportation-stansted-actvists [Last accessed November 3, 2019].

Iregui, Ana María. 2005. "Efficiency Gains from the Elimination of Global Restrictions on Labour Mobility." In *Poverty, International Migration and Asylum*, edited by George J. Borjas and Jeff Crisp, 211–38. New York: Palgrave Macmillan.

Isin, Engin F., and Greg Marc Nielsen, eds. 2008. *Acts of Citizenship.* London; New York: Zed Books Ltd.; Distributed in the USA by Palgrave Macmillan.

Jacobsen, K. 1997. "Refugees' Environmental Impact: The Effect of Patterns of Settlement." *Journal of Refugee Studies* 10 (1): 19–36. https://doi.org/10.1093/jrs/10.1.19.

Jacobson, Matthew Frye. 2002. *Whiteness of a Different Color: European Immigrants and the Alchemy of Race*, 6. Print. Cambridge, MA: Harvard University Press.

Johnson, Corey, Reece Jones, Anssi Paasi, Louise Amoore, Alison Mountz, Mark Salter, and Chris Rumford. 2011. "Interventions on Rethinking 'the Border' in Border Studies." *Political Geography* 30 (2): 61–69. https://doi.org/10.1016/j.polgeo.2011.01.002.

Johnson, Kevin R. 1996–1997. "'Aliens' and the U.S. Immigration Laws: The Social and Legal Construction of Nonpersons." *The University of Miami Inter-American Law Review* 28 (2): 263–92.

Johnson, Kevin R. 2005. "The Forgotten 'Repatriation' of Persons of Mexican Ancestry and Lessons for the 'War on Terror.'" *Pace Law Review* 26: 101–29.

Jones, Reece, ed. 2019. *Open Borders: In Defense of Free Movement*. Geographies of Justice and Social Transformation Series. Athens: University of Georgia Press.

Jones, Reece. 2016. *Violent Borders: Refugees and the Right to Move*. London; New York: Verso.

Jones, Reece, and Corey Johnson, eds. 2014. *Placing the Border in Everyday Life*. Border Regions Series. Farnham, Surrey, England; Burlington, VT: Ashgate Publishing Limited.

Joppke, Christian. 2005. *Selecting by Origin: Ethnic Migration in the Liberal State*. Cambridge, MA: Harvard University Press.

Kaufmann, Eric P. December 21, 2018. "The Myth of White Exceptionalism." *The Spectator*. https://blogs.spectator.co.uk/2018/12/the-myth-of-white-exceptionalism/.

Kaufmann, Eric P. 2019. *Whiteshift: Populism, Immigration and the Future of White Majorities* New York, NY: Abrams Press.

Kelley, Colin P., Shahrzad Mohtadi, Mark A. Cane, Richard Seager, and Yochanan Kushnir. 2015. "Climate Change in the Fertile Crescent and Implications of the Recent Syrian Drought." *Proceedings of the National Academy of Sciences* 112 (11): 3241–46. https://doi.org/10.1073/pnas.1421533112.

Kennan, John. 2013. "Open Borders." *Review of Economic Dynamics* 16 (2): L1–13. https://doi.org/10.1016/j.red.2012.08.003.

Kesler, Christel, and Irene Bloemraad. 2010. "Does Immigration Erode Social Capital? The Conditional Effects of Immigration-Generated Diversity on Trust, Membership, and Participation across 19 Countries, 1981–2000." *Canadian Journal of Political Science/Revue Canadienne De Science Politique* 43 (2): 319–47.

King, Natasha. 2016. *No Borders: The Politics of Immigration Control and Resistance*. London: Zed Books.

Kingsley, Patrick. April 22, 2018. "By Stifling Migration, Sudan's Feared Secret Police Aid Europe." *The New York Times*. https://www.nytimes.com/2018/04/22/world/africa/migration-european-union-sudan.html.

Kingston, Lindsey. 2019. *Fully Human: Personhood, Citizenship, and Rights*. New York: Oxford University Press.

Kirk, Ashley. January 21, 2016. "Mapped: Which Country Has the Most Immigrants?" *The Telegraph*. http://www.telegraph.co.uk/news/worldnews/middleeast/12111108/Mapped-Which-country-has-the-most-immigrants.html.

Kirkup, James, and Robert Winnett. May 25, 2012. "Theresa May Interview: 'We're Going to Give Illegal Migrants a Really Hostile Reception.'" *The Telegraph* https://www.telegraph.co.uk/news/uknews/immigration/9291483/Theresa-May-interview-Were-going-to-give-illegal-migrants-a-really-hostile-reception.html [Last accessed November 3, 2019]

Kopan, Tal. February 28, 2017. "What Is VOICE? Trump Highlights Crimes by Undocumented Immigrants." *CNN*. http://www.cnn.com/2017/02/28/politics/donald-trump-voice-victim-reporting/.

Krasner, Stephen D. 1999. *Sovereignty: Organized Hypocrisy*. Princeton, NJ: Princeton University Press.

Krastev, Ivan. 2017. *After Europe*. Philadelphia: University of Pennsylvania Press.

Kteily, Nour, and Emile Bruneau. 2017. "Backlash: The Politics and Real-World Consequences of Minority Group Dehumanization." *Personality and Social Psychology Bulletin* 43 (1): 87–104. doi:10.1177/0146167216675334.

Kukathas, Chandran. 2003. Immigration. In *The Oxford Handbook of Practical Ethics*, edited by Hugh LaFollette, 567–590. New York: Oxford University Press.

Kukathas, Chandran. 2005. "The Case for Open Immigration." In *Contemporary Debates in Applied Ethics*, edited by Andrew Cohen and Christopher Heath Wellman, 207–20. Malden, MA: Blackwell.

Kukathas, Chandran. 2012. "Why Open Borders?" Ethical Perspectives 19 (4): 649–75.

Kukathas, Chandran. 2017. "On David Miller on Immigration Control." *Critical Review of International Social and Political Philosophy* 20 (6): 712–18. https://doi.org/10.1080/13698230.2016.1231833.

Kustov, Alexander, Dillon Laaker, and Cassidy Reller. 2019. "The Stability of Immigration Attitudes: Evidence and Implications." *SSRN Electronic Journal*. https://doi.org/10.2139/ssrn.3322121.

Kymlicka, Will. 2001. Territorial Boundaries: A Liberal Egalitarian Perspective. In *Boundaries and Justice: Diverse Ethical Perspectives*, edited by David Miller and Sohail H. Hashmi. Princeton, NJ: Princeton University Press.

Lafleur, Jean-Michel, and Abdeslam Marfouk. 2017. *Pourquoi l'immigration? 21 Questions Que Se Posent Les Belges Sur Les Migrations Internationales Au XXIe Siècle*. Carrefours. Louvain-La-Neuve: Academia L'Harmattan.

Landgrave, Michelangelo, and Alex Nowrasteh. 2019. "Criminal Immigrants in 2017: Their Numbers, Demographics, and Countries of Origin." 11. Immigration Research and Policy Brief. CATO Institute. https://www.cato.org/publications/immigration-research-policy-brief/criminal-immigrants-2017-their-numbers-demographics.

Legrain, Philippe. 2007. *Immigrants: Your Country Needs Them*. 1st Princeton ed., with a New Preface. Princeton, NJ: Princeton University Press.

Lenard, Patti Tamara. 2010. "Culture, Free Movement, and Open Borders." *The Review of Politics* 72 (04): 627–52. https://doi.org/10.1017/S0034670510000562.

Lenard, P. T., and C. Straehle. 2011. "Temporary Labour Migration, Global Redistribution, and Democratic Justice." *Politics, Philosophy & Economics* 11 (2): 206–30. https://doi.org/10.1177/1470594X10392338.

Lepore, Jill. 2019. *This America: The Case for the Nation*. First ed. New York: Liveright Publishing Corporation.

Levitt, Peggy, and B. Nadya Jaworsky. 2007. "Transnational Migration Studies: Past Developments and Future Trends." *Annual Review of Sociology* 33 (1): 129–56. https://doi.org/10.1146/annurev.soc.33.040406.131816.

Liao, Yiwu. 2009. *The Corpse Walker: Real Life Stories, China from the Bottom Up.* New York, NY: Anchor Books.

Light, Michael T., and Ty Miller. 2018. "Does Undocumented Immigration Increase Violent Crime?" *Criminology* 56 (2): 370–401. https://doi.org/10.1111/1745-9125.12175.

Lima Marín, René, and Danielle C. Jefferis. 2019. "It's Just Like Prison: Is a Civil (Nonpunitive) System of Immigration Detention Theoretically Possible?" *Denver Law Review* 96: 1–17.

Lind, Dara. June 25, 2019. "The Horrifying Conditions Facing Kids in Border Detention, Explained." *Vox.* https://www.vox.com/policy-and-politics/2019/6/25/18715725/children-border-detention-kids-cages-immigration.

Losurdo, Domenico. 2011. *Liberalism: A Counter-History.* Translated by Gregory Elliott. London; New York: Verso Books.

Macedo, Stephen. 2018. "The Moral Dilemma of U.S. Immigration Policy: Open Borders versus Social Justice?" In *Debating Immigration, Second Edition*, edited by Carol M. Swain, 286–310. Cambridge, UK; New York: Cambridge University Press.

Maghularia, Rita, and Silke Uebelmesser. 2019. "Working Paper Do Immigrants Affect Crime? Evidence from Panel Data for Germany." Working Paper 7696. Munich, Germany: CESifo.

Mancilla, Alejandra. 2016. *The Right of Necessity: Moral Cosmopolitanism and Global Poverty.* Off the Fence: Morality, Politics, and Society. London: Rowman & Littlefield International, Ltd.

Manjoo, Farhad. January 16, 2019. "There's Nothing Wrong with Open Borders." *The New York Times*, 2019. https://www.nytimes.com/2019/01/16/opinion/open-borders-immigration.html.

Martén, Linna, Jens Hainmueller, and Dominik Hangartner. 2019. "Ethnic Networks Can Foster the Economic Integration of Refugees." *Proceedings of the National Academy of Sciences*, July, 201820345. https://doi.org/10.1073/pnas.1820345116.

Martin, Philip. 2005. "Economic Costs and Benefits of International Labour Migration." In *World Migration 2005: Costs and Benefits of International Migration*, 185–201. Geneva, Switzerland: IOM Publishers.

Martínez, Oscar. 2013. *The Beast: Riding the Rails and Dodging Narcos on the Migrant Trail.* Translated by Daniela Maria Ugaz and John Washington. London; New York: Verso.

Massey, Douglas S. 2007. *Categorically Unequal: The American Stratification System.* A Russell Sage Foundation Centennial Volume. New York: Russell Sage Foundation.

Massey, Douglas S., Jorge Durand, and Karen A. Pren. 2016. "Why Border Enforcement Backfired." *American Journal of Sociology* 121 (5): 1557–600. https://doi.org/10.1086/684200.

Mathieu, Mathilde, and Rouguyata Sall. July 28, 2019. "The Gilets Noirs Are in the Building." Translated by David Broder. *Jacobin.* https://jacobinmag.com/2019/07/gilets-noirs-france-protesters-sans-papiers.

McKeown, Adam. 2004. "Global Migration 1846–1940." *Journal of World History* 15 (2): 155–89. https://doi.org/10.1353/jwh.2004.0026.

Mendoza, José Jorge. 2016a "Illegal: White Supremacy and Immigration." In *The Ethics and Politics of Immigration: Core Issues and Emerging Trends*, edited by Alex Sager, 201–20. Lanham, MD: Rowman & Littlefield International, 2016.

Mendoza, José Jorge. 2016b. *The Moral and Political Philosophy of Immigration: Liberty, Security, and Equality.* Lanham, MD: Lexington Books.

Menjívar, Cecilia, and Leisy J. Abrego. 2012. "Legal Violence: Immigration Law and the Lives of Central American Immigrants." *American Journal of Sociology* 117 (5): 1380–421. https://doi.org/10.1086/663575.

Messing, Vera, and Bence Ságvári. 2019. *Still Divided but More Open: Mapping European Attitudes towards Migration before and after the Migration Crisis.* http://library.fes.de/pdf-files/bueros/budapest/15322.pdf.

Metcalfe, David. July 8, 2019. "If There Is a 'Native' Language of Britain, Boris Johnson, It Certainly Isn't English." *The Guardian.* https://www.theguardian.com/politics/2019/jul/08/if-there-is-a-native-language-of-britain-boris-johnson-it-certainly-isnt-english.

Mignolo, Walter. 2011. *The Darker Side of Western Modernity: Global Futures, Decolonial Options.* Latin America Otherwise: Languages, Empires, Nations. Durham, NC: Duke University Press.

Migration and Refugee Services/United States Conference of Catholic Bishops, and Center for Migration Studies. 2015. "Unlocking Human Dignity: A Plan to Transform the U.S. Immigrant Detention System." http://www.usccb.org/about/migration-and-refugee-services/upload/unlocking-human-dignity.pdf.

Milanovic, Branko. 2013. "Global Income Inequality in Numbers: In History and Now." *Global Policy* 4 (2): 198–208. https://doi.org/10.1111/1758-5899.12032.

Miller, David. 2005. "Immigration: The Case for Limits." In *Contemporary Debates in Applied Ethics*, edited by Andrew Cohen and Christopher Heath Wellman, 193–206. Malden, MA: Blackwell.

Miller, David. 2007. *National Responsibility and Global Justice.* New York, NY: Oxford University Press.

Miller, David. 2010. "Why Immigration Controls Are Not Coercive: A Reply to Arash Abizadeh." *Political Theory* 38 (1): 111–20. https://doi.org/10.1177/0090591709348194.

Miller, David. 2016. *Strangers in Our Midst: The Political Philosophy of Immigration.* Cambridge, MA: Harvard University Press.

Miller, Michael K., and Margaret E. Peters. 2018. "Restraining the Huddled Masses: Migration Policy and Autocratic Survival." *British Journal of Political Science* (March): 1–31. https://doi.org/10.1017/S0007123417000680.

Mills Rodrigo, Charles. July 24, 2019. "US Citizen Accuses CBP of 'inhumane' Treatment While in Custody." *The Hill.* https://thehill.com/latino/454648-us-citizen-accuses-cbp-of-inhumane-treatment-while-in-custody.

Miron, Jeffrey. July 2018. "Forget the Wall Already, It's Time for the U.S. to Have Open Borders." *USA Today.* https://www.usatoday.com/story/opinion/2018/07/31/open-borders-help-economy-combat-illegal-immigration-column/862185002/.

Mongia, Radhika Viyas. 2018. *Indian Migration and Empire: A Colonial Genealogy of the Modern State.* Durham, NC: Duke University Press.

Morin, Rebecca. April 8, 2019. "Bernie Sanders Says He Does Not Support Open Borders." *Politico.* https://www.politico.com/story/2019/04/08/bernie-sanders-open-borders-1261392.

Moses, Jonathon Wayne. 2006. *International Migration: Globalization's Last Frontier.* Global Issues. New York: Zed Books.

Moses, Jonathon W., and Letnes Bjørn. 2005. "Efficiency Gains from the Elimination of Global Restrictions on Labour Mobility." In *Poverty, International Migration and Asylum,* edited by George J. Borjas and Jeff Crisp, 188–210. New York: Palgrave Macmillan.

Mulvey, G. 2010. "When Policy Creates Politics: The Problematizing of Immigration and the Consequences for Refugee Integration in the UK." *Journal of Refugee Studies* 23 (4): 437–62. https://doi.org/10.1093/jrs/feq045.

Muradian, Roldan. 2006. "Immigration and the Environment: Underlying Values and Scope of Analysis." *Ecological Economics* 59 (2): 208–13. https://doi.org/10.1016/j.ecolecon.2005.11.036.

Murray, Douglas. 2017. *The Strange Death of Europe: Immigration, Identity, Islam.* London: Bloomsbury Continuum, an imprint of Bloomsbury Publishing Plc.

Nandita, Sharma, and Cynthia Wright. 2008. "Decolonizing Resistance, Challenging Colonial States." *Social Justice* 35 (3): 120–38.

Nathanson, Rebecca. November 17, 2017. "These Activists Blocked Migrant Deportations. Now They Face Life Imprisonment in the U.K." *The Intercept.* https://theintercept.com/2018/11/17/stansted-deportation-flights-uk/.

National Academies of Sciences, Engineering, and Medicine. 2017. *The Economic and Fiscal Consequences of Immigration,* edited by Francine D. Blau and Christopher Mackie. Washington, D.C.: National Academies Press. https://doi.org/10.17226/23550.

National Domestic Workers Alliance. 2012. "Home Economics: The Invisible and Unregulated World of Domestic Work." New York: Center for Urban Economic Development, University of Illinois at Chicago. http://www.idwfed.org/en/resources/home-economics-the-invisible-and-unregulated-world-of-domestic-work/@@display-file/attachment_1.

Nethery, Amy, and Stephanie Jessica Silverman, eds. 2015. *Immigration Detention: The Migration of a Policy and Its Human Impact.* London; New York: Routledge.

Neuman, Gerald L. 1994–1995. "Aliens as Outlaws: Government Services, Proposition 187, and the Structure of Equal Protection." *University of California Los Angeles Law Review* 1425: 1425–52.

Newman, David. 2006. "The Lines That Continue to Separate Us: Borders in Our 'Borderless' World." *Progress in Human Geography* 30 (2): 143–61. https://doi.org/10.1191/0309132506ph599xx.

Ngai, Mae M. 2004. *Impossible Subjects: Illegal Aliens and the Making of Modern America.* Princeton, NJ: Princeton University Press.

Nossiter, Adam. January 5, 2017. "Farmer on Trial Defends Smuggling Migrants: 'I Am a Frenchman.'" *The New York Times.* http://www.nytimes.com/2017/01/05/world/europe/cedric-herrou-migrant-smuggler-trial-france.html?smid=tw-share&_r=0.

Novak, Paolo. 2017. "Back to Borders." *Critical Sociology* 43 (6): 847–64. https://doi.org/10.1177/0896920516644034.

Nussbaum, Martha Craven. 2019. *The Cosmopolitan Tradition: A Noble but Flawed Ideal*. Cambridge, Massachusetts: The Belknap Press of Harvard University Press.

Nyers, Peter. 2003. "Abject Cosmopolitanism: The Politics of Protection in the Anti-Deportation Movement." *Third World Quarterly* 24 (6): 1069–93.

Oberman, Kieran. 2011. "Immigration, Global Poverty and the Right to Stay." *Political Studies* 59 (2): 253–68. https://doi.org/10.1111/j.1467-9248.2011.00889.x.

Oberman, Kieran. 2013. "Can Brain Drain Justify Immigration Restrictions?" *Ethics* 123 (3): 427–55. https://doi.org/10.1086/669567.

Oberman, Kieran. 2015. "Poverty and Immigration Policy." *American Political Science Review* 109 (02): 239–51. https://doi.org/10.1017/S0003055415000106.

Oberman, Kieran. 2016. "Immigration as a Human Right." In *Migration in Political Theory: The Ethics of Movement and Membership*, edited by Sarah Fine and Lea Ypi, 32–56. Oxford: Oxford University Press.

Ochoa Espejo, Paulina. 2016. "Taking Place Seriously: Territorial Presence and the Rights of Immigrants." *Journal of Political Philosophy* 24 (1): 67–87. https://doi.org/10.1111/jopp.12061.

Office of the High Commission for Human Rights. 1999. "CCPR General Comment No. 27: Article 12 (Freedom of Movement)." https://www.refworld.org/pdfid/45139c394.pdf.

Office of the Inspector General. 2019. "Management Alert—DHS Needs to Address Dangerous Overcrowding among Single Adults at El Paso Del Norte Processing Center." OIG-19-46. U.S. Department of Homeland Security. https://www.oig.dhs.gov/sites/default/files/assets/2019-05/OIG-19-46-May19.pdf.

Okin, Susan Moller. 1999. *Is Multiculturalism Bad for Women?* Princeton, N.J: Princeton University Press.

Okrent, Daniel. 2019. *The Guarded Gate: Bigotry, Eugenics, and the Law That Kept Two Generations of Jews, Italians, and Other European Immigrants out of America*. New York: Scribner.

Orgad, Li'av. 2015. *The Cultural Defense of Nations: A Liberal Theory of Majority Rights*. First ed. Oxford Constitutional Theory. Oxford, UK; New York: Oxford University Press.

Orgad, Li'av, and Theodore Ruthizer. 2010. "Race, Religion and Nationality in Immigration Selection: 120 Years after the Chinese Exclusion Case." *Constitutional Commentary* 26: 237–96.

Organization for Economic Cooperation and Development. 2013. "The Fiscal Impact of Immigration in OECD Countries." In *International Migration Outlook 2013*, 125–89. Paris: OECD.

Ottaviano, Gianmarco I. P., and Giovanni Peri. 2012. "Rethinking the Effects of Immigration Wages." *Journal of the European Economic Association* 10 (1): 152–97. https://doi.org/10.1111/j.1542-4774.2011.01052.x.

Ousey, Graham C., and Charis E. Kubrin. 2018. "Immigration and Crime: Assessing a Contentious Issue." *Annual Review of Criminology* 1 (1): 63–84. https://doi.org/10.1146/annurev-criminol-032317-092026.

Parekh, Bhikhu. 2002. *Rethinking Multiculturalism: Cultural Diversity and Political Theory*. Cambridge: Harvard University press.

Parker, Noel, and Nick Vaughan-Williams. 2009. "Lines in the Sand? Towards an Agenda for Critical Border Studies." *Geopolitics* 14 (3): 582–87. https://doi.org/10.1080/14650040903081297.

Parker, Noel, and Nick Vaughan-Williams. 2012. "Critical Border Studies: Broadening and Deepening the 'Lines in the Sand Agenda.'" *Geopolitics* 17 (4): 727–33. https://doi.org/10.1080/14650045.2012.706111.

Passel, Jeffrey S., and D'Vera Cohn. 2016. "Overall Number of U.S. Unauthorized Immigrants Holds Steady Since 2009." Pew Research Center. http://www.pewhispanic.org/2016/09/20/overall-number-of-u-s-unauthorized-immigrants-holds-steady-since-2009/.

Pécoud, Antoine, and Paul de Guchteneire. 2006. "International Migration, Border Controls and Human Rights: Assessing the Relevance of a Right to Mobility." *Journal of Borderlands Studies* 21 (6): 69–86.

Penn, Ben. June 24, 2019. "Human Trafficking Victims Blocked from Visas by Trump Wage Boss." *Bloomberg Law*. https://news.bloomberglaw.com/daily-labor-report/human-trafficking-victims-blocked-from-visas-by-trump-wage-boss.

Pettigrew, Thomas F., and Linda R. Tropp. 2006. "A Meta-Analytic Test of Intergroup Contact Theory." *Journal of Personality and Social Psychology* 90 (5): 751–83. https://doi.org/10.1037/0022-3514.90.5.751.

Pevnick, Ryan. 2009. "Social Trust and the Ethics of Immigration Policy." *Journal of Political Philosophy* 17 (2): 146–67. https://doi.org/10.1111/j.1467-9760.2007.00296.x.

Pevnick, Ryan. 2011. *Immigration and the Constraints of Justice: Between Open Borders and Absolute Sovereignty*. Cambridge, UK; New York: Cambridge University Press.

Pew Research Center. 2011. *Muslim Americans: No Signs of Growth in Alienation or Support for Extremism*. Washington, D.C.: Pew Research Center. http://www.people-press.org/2011/08/30/muslim-americans-no-signs-of-growth-in-alienation-or-support-for-extremism.

Pew Research Center. 2017. *Origins and Destinations of European Union Migrants within the EU*. Washington, D.C.: Pew Research Center. http://www.pewglobal.org/interactives/origins-destinations-of-european-union-migrants-within-the-eu/.

Phillips, Kristine. 2017. "Thousands of ICE Detainees Claim They Were Forced into Labor, a Violation of Anti-Slavery Laws." *Washington Post*, March 5, 2017. https://www.washingtonpost.com/news/post-nation/wp/2017/03/05/thousands-of-ice-detainees-claim-they-were-forced-into-labor-a-violation-of-anti-slavery-laws/.

Pirie, Sophie H. 1990. "The Origins of a Political Trial: The Sanctuary Movement and Political Justice." *Yale Journal of Law & the Humanities* 2 (2): 381–416.

Pogge, Thomas. 1997. *"Migration and Poverty." In Citizenship and Exclusion,* edited by Veit-Michael Bader, 12–27. Houndmills; New York: Macmillan Press; St. Martin's Press.

Popova, Natalia, and Mustafa Hakki Özel. 2018. *"ILO Global Estimates on International Migrant Workers: Results and Methodology."* Geneva, Switzerland: International Labour Office.

Prendergast, Curt. March 1, 2019. "Border Aid Volunteers Sentenced to Probation in Tucson." *Arizona Daily Star*. https://tucson.com/news/local/border-aid-volunteers-sentenced-to-probation-in-tucson/article_1160a3c2-3c74-11e9-bd57-873b4471925b.html.

Pritchett, Lant. 2006. *Let Their People Come: Breaking the Gridlock on International Labor Mobility*. Washington, D.C.: Center for Global Development.

Puckett, Lily. July 26, 2019. "US Teenager Detained at Border Lost 26 Pounds in a Month: 'It Was Inhumane How They Treated Us.'" *The Independent*. https://www.independent.co.uk/news/world/americas/francisco-erwin-galicia-us-border-immigration-teenager-weight-loss-cbp-a9022911.html.

Putnam, Robert D. 2001. *Bowling Alone: The Collapse and Revival of American Community*. New York: Simon & Schuster.

Putnam, Robert D. 2007. "E Pluribus Unum: Diversity and Community in the Twenty-First Century the 2006 Johan Skytte Prize Lecture." *Scandinavian Political Studies* 30 (2): 137–74. https://doi.org/10.1111/j.1467-9477.2007.00176.x.

Rancière, Jacques. 1999. *Disagreement: Politics and Philosophy*. Minneapolis: University of Minnesota Press.

Raspail, Jean. 1975. *The Camp of the Saints*. Translated by Norman Shapiro. New York: Charles Schibner's Sons.

Rawls, John. 1999. *Theory of Justice: Revised Edition*. Cambridge, MA: Harvard University Press.

Read, Rupert. June 19, 2014. "Love Immigrants, Rather Than Large-Scale Immigration." *Ecologist: The Journal for the Post-Industrial Age*. https://theecologist.org/2014/jun/19/love-immigrants-rather-large-scale-immigration.

Riley, Jason. 2008. *Let Them in: The Case for Open Borders*. New York: Gotham Books.

Roediger, David R. 2006. *Working toward Whiteness: How America's Immigrants Became White; the Strange Journey from Ellis Island to the Suburbs*. Paperback ed. New York: Basic Books.

Rosenblum, Marc R. 2010. "Immigrant Legalization in the United States and European Union: Policy Goals and Program Design." Policy Brief. Washington, D.C.: Migration Policy Institute. https://www.migrationpolicy.org/research/immigrant-legalization-united-states-and-european-union.

Roser, Max. December 2017. "Fertility Rate." *Our World in Data*. https://ourworldindata.org/fertility-rate.

Ruark, Eric, and Jack Martin. 2009. *The Sinking Lifeboat: Uncontrolled Immigration and the U.S. Health Care System in 2009*. Washington, D.C.: Federation for American Immigration Reform. http://www.fairus.org/site/DocServer/healthcare_09.pdf?docID=3521.

Ruhs, Martin. 2013. *The Price of Rights: Regulating International Labor Migration*. Princeton, NJ: Princeton University Press.

Rumford, C. 2006. "Theorizing Borders." *European Journal of Social Theory* 9 (2): 155–69. https://doi.org/10.1177/1368431006063330.

Sager, Alex. 2012. "Review: Ryan Pevnick, Immigration and the Constraints of Justice." *Journal of Politics* 74 (3).

Sager, Alex. 2012a. "Immigration, Class, and Global Justice: Some Moral Considerations/Implications." In *La Communauté Politique En Question. Regards Croisés Sur l'immigration, La Citoyenneté, La Diversité et Le Pouvoir*, edited by Micheline Labelle, Jocelyne Couture, and Frank Remiggi. Quebec: UQAM Press.

Sager, Alex. 2012b. "Immigration and the Constraints of Justice: Between Open Borders and Absolute Sovereignty. By Ryan Pevnick. (Cambridge University

Press, 2011)." *The Journal of Politics* 74 (3): E35. https://doi.org/10.1017/S0022 381612000291.

Sager, Alex. 2014. "Reframing the Brain Drain." *Critical Review of International Social and Political Philosophy* 17 (5): 560–79. https://doi.org/10.1080/1369823 0.2014.919061.

Sager, Alex. 2016a. "Methodological Nationalism, Migration and Political Theory." *Political Studies* 64 (1): 42–59.

Sager, Alex. 2016b. "Methodological Nationalism and the 'Brain Drain.'" In *The Ethics and Politics of Immigration: Core Issues and Emerging Trends*, edited by Alex Sager. Lanham, MD: Rowman & Littlefield International.

Sager, Alex. 2017. "Immigration Enforcement and Domination: An Indirect Argument for Much More Open Borders." *Political Research Quarterly* 70 (1): 42–54. https://doi.org/10.1177/1065912916680036.

Sager, Alex. 2018a. "Ethics and Migration Crises." In *The Handbook of Migration Crises*, edited by Cecilia Menjívar, Immanuel Ness, and Marie Ruiz. New York: Oxford University Press.

Sager, Alex. 2018b. "Reclaiming Cosmopolitanism through Migrant Protests." In Migration, Protest Movements and the Politics of Resistance. *A Radical Political Philosophy of Cosmopolitanism*, edited by Tamara Caraus and Elena Paris, 171–85. New York, NY: Routledge.

Sager, Alex. 2018c. *Toward a Cosmopolitan Ethics of Mobility: The Migrant's-Eye View of the World*. Mobility & Politics 14800. New York: Springer Science+ Business Media.

Sager, Alex. Forthcoming. "The Uses and Abuses of 'Migrant Crisis.'" In *Immigrants and Refugees in Times of Crisis*, edited by Theodoros Fouskas. European Public Law Organization.

Salant, Brian. 2016. "Top 10 of 2016—Issue #10: While Mobility Comes under Assault in Europe, Other Regions Forge Ahead." Migration Policy Institute. http://www.migrationpolicy.org/article/top-10-2016-issue-10-while-mobility-comes-under-assault-europe-other-regions-forge-ahead.

Sanchez, Gabriella E. 2015. *Human Smuggling and Border Crossings*. Routledge Studies in Criminal Justice, Borders and Citizenship. London; New York: Routledge.

Sanchez, Gabriella. 2019. "Women and Migrant Smuggling Facilitation in the United States." In *Critical Insights on Irregular Migration Facilitation: Global Perspectives*, edited by Gabriella Sanchez and Luigi Achilli, 33–36. Florence: European University Institute. https://cadmus.eui.eu/handle/1814/62384.

Sandelind, Clara. March 2019. "Can the Welfare State Justify Restrictive Asylum Policies? A Critical Approach." *Ethical Theory and Moral Practice*. https://doi.org/10.1007/s10677-019-09989-3.

Sassen, Saskia. 1988. *The Mobility of Labor and Capital: A Study in International Investment and Labor Flow*. Cambridge, UK; New York: Cambridge University Press.

Sassen, S. 2008. "Two Stops in Today's New Global Geographies: Shaping Novel Labor Supplies and Employment Regimes." *American Behavioral Scientist* 52 (3): 457–96. https://doi.org/10.1177/0002764208325312.

Scheffler, Samuel. 2007. "Immigration and the Significance of Culture." *Philosophy & Public Affairs* 35 (2): 93–125.

Scott, James C. 1987. *Weapons of the Weak: Everyday Forms of Peasant Resistance.* New Haven, CT: Yale University Press.

Scott, James C. 1990. *Domination and the Arts of Resistance: Hidden Transcripts.* New Haven, CT: Yale University Press.

Seglow, Jonathan. 2005. "The Ethics of Immigration." *Political Studies Review* 3 (3): 317–34. https://doi.org/10.1111/j.1478-9299.2005.00026.x.

Sen, Amartya. 1999. "Democracy as a Universal Value." *Journal of Democracy* 10 (3): 3–17.

Serwer, Adam. April 2019. "White Nationalism's Deep American Roots." *The Atlantic.* https://www.theatlantic.com/magazine/archive/2019/04/adam-serwer-madison-grant-white-nationalism/583258/.

Shachar, Ayelet. 2009. *The Birthright Lottery: Citizenship and Global Inequality.* Cambridge, MA: Harvard University Press.

Sharma, Nandita. 2005. "Anti-Trafficking Rhetoric and the Making of a Global Apartheid." *NWSA Journal* 17 (3): 88–11.

Shumsky, Neil Larry. 2008. "Noah Webster and the Invention of Immigration." *The New England Quarterly* 81 (1): 126–35.

Sidgwick, Henry. 1897. *The Elements of Politics.* Second ed. London: MacMillan and Co., Limited.

Siegfried, Kristy. June 30, 2016. "Europe Tries to Buy Its Way Out of the Migration Crisis." *The New Humanitarian.* http://www.thenewhumanitarian.org/analysis/2016/06/30/europe-tries-buy-its-way-out-migration-crisis

Silverman, Stephanie J., and Amy Nethery. 2015. "Detention and Its Human Impact." In *Immigration Detention: The Migration of a Policy and Its Human Impact*, edited by Amy Nethery and Stephanie Jessica Silverman, 1–12. London; New York: Routledge.

Skeldon, Ronald. 1997. *Migration and Development: A Global Perspective.* Harlow: Longman.

Slack, Jeremy, Daniel E. Martínez, Alison Elizabeth Lee, and Scott Whiteford. 2016. "The Geography of Border Militarization: Violence, Death and Health in Mexico and the United States." *Journal of Latin American Geography* 15 (1): 7–32. https://doi.org/10.1353/lag.2016.0009.

Smith, Christian. 2016. "The Conceptual Incoherence of 'Culture' in American Sociology." *The American Sociologist* 47 (4): 388–415. https://doi.org/10.1007/s12108-016-9308-y.

Smith, Rogers M. 1997. *Civil Ideals: Conflicting Visions of Citizenship in U.S. History.* New Haven, CT; and London: Yale University Press.

Steiner, Hillel. 2001. "Hard Borders, Compensation, and Classical Liberalism." In *Boundaries and Justice: Diverse Ethical Perspectives*, edited by David Miller and Sohail H. Hashmi, 79–88. Princeton, NJ: Princeton University Press.

Stumpf, Julliet. 2006. "The Crimmigration Crisis: Immigrants, Crime, and Sovereign Power." *American University Law Review* 56 (2): 367–419.

Sturgis, Patrick, Ian Brunton-Smith, Sanna Read, and Nick Allum. 2011. "Does Ethnic Diversity Erode Trust? Putnam's 'Hunkering Down' Thesis Reconsidered." *British*

Journal of Political Science 41 (1) (January): 57–82. https://doi.org/10.1017/S0007123410000281.

Suliman, Baldo. 2017. "Border Control from Hell: How the EU's Migration Partnership Legitimizes Sudan's 'Militia State.'" The Enough Project, https://enoughproject.org/reports/border-control-hell-how-eus-migration-partnership-legitimizes-sudans-militia-state [Last accessed November 3, 2019].

Sweney, Mark. April 12, 2018. "BBC under Fire over Enoch Powell 'Rivers of Blood' Broadcast." *The Guardian.* https://www.theguardian.com/media/2018/apr/12/bbc-to-air-reading-of-enoch-powells-rivers-of-blood-speech.

Tamir, Yael. 2019. *Why Nationalism.* Princeton, NJ: Princeton University Press.

Tessler, Mark. 2003. "Arab and Muslim Political Attitudes: Stereotypes and Evidence from Survey Research." *International Studies Perspectives* 4 (2): 175–81. https://doi.org/10.1111/1528-3577.402005.

Thompson, Ginger. July 16, 2019. "A Border Patrol Agent Reveals What It's Really Like to Guard Migrant Children." *ProPublica.* https://www.propublica.org/article/a-border-patrol-agent-reveals-what-its-really-like-to-guard-migrant-children.

Tilly, Charles. 1999. *Durable Inequality.* Berkeley: University of California Press.

Torpey, John. 2000. *The Invention of the Passport: Surveillance, Citizenship, and the State.* Cambridge Studies in Law and Society. Cambridge, UK; New York: Cambridge University Press.

United Nations Support Mission in Libya. 2016. "Detained and Dehumanised: Report on Human Rights Abuses against Migrants in Libya." United Nations Human Rights. https://unsmil.unmissions.org/Portals/unsmil/Documents/Migrants%20report-EN.pdf.

United Nations Support Mission in Libya. 2018. "Desperate and Dangerous: Report on the Human Rights Situation of Migrants and Refugees in Libya." United Nations Human Rights. https://www.ohchr.org/Documents/Countries/LY/LibyaMigrationReport.pdf.

Vallet, Élisabeth, and Charles-Philippe David. 2012. "Introduction: The (Re)Building of the Wall in International Relations." *Journal of Borderlands Studies* 27 (2): 111–19. doi:10.1080/08865655.2012.687211.

Vertovec, Steven. 2007. "Super-Diversity and Its Implications." *Ethnic and Racial Studies* 30 (6): 1024–54. https://doi.org/10.1080/01419870701599465.

Volpp, Leti. 2001. "Feminism versus Multiculturalism." *Columbia Law Review* 101 (5): 1181–218.

Walia, Harsha. 2013. *Undoing Border Imperialism.* Anarchist Interventions 06. Oakland, CA: Washington, D.C.: AK Press; Institute for Anarchist Studies.

Walters, William. 2011. "Foucault and Frontiers: Notes on the Humanitarian Border." In *Governmentality: Current Issues and Future Challenges*, edited by Ulrich Bröckling, Susanne Krasmann, and Thomas Lemke, 138–64. Routledge Studies in Social and Political Thought 71. New York: Routledge.

Walzer, Michael. 1983. *Spheres of Justice: A Defense of Pluralism and Equality.* New York: Basic Books.

Wang, Hansi Lo, Alyson Hurt, and Camila Domonoske. March 8, 2017. "How America's Idea of Illegal Immigration Doesn't Always Match Reality." *NPR.*

http://www.npr.org/sections/thetwo-way/2017/03/08/517561046/how-americas-idea-of-illegal-immigration-doesnt-always-match-reality.

Wang, Xia. 2012. "Undocumented Immigrants as Perceived Criminal Threat: A Test of the Minority Threat Perspective." *Criminology* 50 (3): 743–76. https://doi.org/10.1111/j.1745-9125.2012.00278.x.

Washington, John. April 24, 2019. "What Would an Open-Borders World Actually Look Like?" *The Nation*. https://www.thenation.com/article/open-borders-immigration-asylum-refugees/.

Wellman, Christopher Heath. 2008. "Immigration and Freedom of Association." *Ethics* 119 (1): 109–41. https://doi.org/10.1086/592311.

Wellman, Christopher Heath. 2015. "Immigration." In *The Stanford Encyclopedia of Philosophy*, edited by Edward N. Zalta. https://plato.stanford.edu/archives/sum2015/entries/immigration/ [Last accessed October 30, 2019].

Wellman, Christopher Heath, and Phillip Cole. 2011. *Debating the Ethics of Immigration: Is There a Right to Exclude?* Debating Ethics. Oxford: Oxford University Press.

Wheeler, William. July 21, 2014. "How Not to Design a World without Borders." *The Atlantic*. https://www.theatlantic.com/international/archive/2014/07/how-not-to-design-a-world-without-borders/374563/.

White House. 2018a. "Facing the Facts about Our Broken Immigration System." https://www.whitehouse.gov/briefings-statements/facing-facts-broken-immigration-system/.

White House. 2018b. "President Donald J. Trump Is Acting to Enforce the Law, While Keeping Families Together." https://www.whitehouse.gov/briefings-statements/president-donald-j-trump-acting-enforce-law-keeping-families-together/.

White, Stuart. 1997. "Freedom of Association and the Right to Exclude." *Journal of Political Philosophy* 5 (4): 373–91. https://doi.org/10.1111/1467-9760.00039.

Wickes, Rebecca, and Michael Sydes. 2018. "Immigration and Crime." In *The Routledge Handbook on Crime and International Migration*, edited by Sharon Pickering and Julie Ham, 11–25. London, United Kingdom: Routledge.

Wilcox, Shelly. 2004. "Culture, National Identity, and Admission to Citizenship." *Social Theory and Practice* 30 (4): 559–83.

Wilcox, Shelley. 2009. "The Open Borders Debate on Immigration." *Philosophy Compass* 4 (5): 813–21. https://doi.org/10.1111/j.1747-9991.2009.00230.x.

Wilcox, Shelley. 2012. "Review of Immigration and the Constraints of Justice: Between Borders and Absolute Sovereignty." *Ethics* 122: 617–22.

Wimmer, Andreas, and Nina Glick Schiller. 2002. "Methodological Nationalism and beyond: Nation-State Building, Migration and the Social Sciences." *Global Networks* 2 (4): 301–34. https://doi.org/10.1111/1471-0374.00043.

Wimmer, Andres, and Nina Glick Schiller. 2003. "Methodological Nationalism, the Social Sciences, and the Study of Migration: An Essay in Historical Epistemology." *International Migration Review* 37 (3): 576–610.

Wintor, Patrick. November 22, 2018. "Hillary Clinton: Europe Must Curb Immigration to Stop Rightwing Populists." *The Guardian*. https://www.theguardian.com/world/2018/nov/22/hillary-clinton-europe-must-curb-immigration-stop-populists-trump-brexit.

Wong, Tom K. 2017. "The Effects of Sanctuary Policies on Crime and the Economy." Center for American Progress. https://www.americanprogress.org/issues/immigra tion/reports/2017/01/26/297366/the-effects-of-sanctuary-policies-on-crime-and-the-economy/.

Wong, Tom K., Deborah Kang, Carolina Valdivia, Josefina Espino, Michelle Gonzalez, and Elia Peralta. 2019. "How Interior Immigration Enforcement Affects Trust in Law Enforcement." Working Paper 2. La Jolla, CA: U.S. Immigration Policy Center.

World Bank. 2005. *Global Economic Prospects: Economic Implications of Remittances and Migration.* Washington, D.C.

Yglesias, Matthew. June 22, 2018. "The Pernicious Myth of 'Open Borders.'" *Vox.* https://www.vox.com/2018/6/22/17488272/open-borders-myth.

Žižek, Slavoj. 2016. *Against the Double Blackmail: Refugees, Terror and Other Troubles with the Neighbours.* London: Allen Lane.

Zolberg, Aristide R. 2012. "Why Not the Whole World? Ethical Dilemmas of Immigration Policy." *American Behavioral Scientist* 56 (9): 1204–22. https://doi. org/10.1177/0002764212443821.

Index

About the Author

Alex Sager is associate professor of philosophy and university studies at Portland State University, Oregon, USA. He is the author of *Toward a Cosmopolitan Theory of Mobility: The Migrant's Eye-View of the World* (Palgrave Pivot 2018) and editor of *The Ethics and Politics of Immigration: Core Issues and Emerging Trends* (Rowman & Littlefield International 2016).